# The Maisel's Murals Restored

Mural Photographs by Paul R. Secord

© 2020

All Rights Reserved

No part of this book may be reproduced in any form or by any electronic or mechanical means including information storage and retrieval systems without permission in writing from the publisher, except by a reviewer who may quote brief passages in a review.
Secord books are available through Amazon.com

Library of Congress Cataloging-in-Publication Data Names: Secord, Paul R., Author (1950 - )
Title: The Maisel Murals Restored / by Paul R. Secord.
Description: Santa Fe : Secord Press, 2020. Includes bibliographical references.
Identifiers: ISBN: 9798550995327  LCCN: 2020921209
Subjects (LCSH):
- Mural painting and decoration, American-New Mexico-Albuquerque-20th century.
- Indian mural painting and decoration-New Mexico-Albuquerque-20th century.
- Maisel's Indian Trading Post (Albuquerque, N.M.) I Indians in art.
- Rites and ceremonies in art.
- Group work in art-New Mexico-Albuquerque-History-20th century.
- Rush, Olive, 1873-1966.

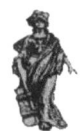

Secord Books
7737 Cedar Canyon Road NE
Albuquerque, New Mexico
87122 - 1628
psecord@earthlink.net

# DEDICATION

My 2018 book *The Maisel's Murals 1939* is dedicated to each of the eleven Native American Artists who painted the Maisel's Murals. That prior dedication holds true for this book as well. I would like to add Maurice M. Maisel for his vision in allowing his storefront to be a showcase of Native American art at its best. He let the art speak for itself and stayed out of the way. To architect John G. Meem for supporting and facilitating the storefront's Native American art presentation. And lastly to Olive Rush for coordinating the execution of a truly magnificent project that in one place presents the best of Southwest Native American art of the time.

# TABLE OF CONTENTS

Forward ................................................................................................................. 1
Introduction: ......................................................................................................... 2
Chapter One: How This Book Came About ....................................................... 3
Chapter Two: Virtual Restoration ....................................................................... 4
Chapter Three: *The Studio* Style ....................................................................... 7
Chapter Four: The Artists .................................................................................... 8
Chapter Five: Painting the Murals ..................................................................... 11
Chapter Six: Overall Considerations ................................................................. 12
    1: Common Characteristics .............................................................................. 13
    2: First and Second Generation Artists ............................................................ 13
    3: Creativity Through Constraint ..................................................................... 13
    4: Precision and Detail .................................................................................... 14
    5: Movement .................................................................................................... 16
    6: Men and Women ......................................................................................... 17
    7: Resistance .................................................................................................... 18
    8 Engaging the Viewer .................................................................................... 19
    9: Kitsch - When Art Becomes Banal .............................................................. 20
Chapter Seven: A Unified Design Conception .................................................. 22
Chapter Eight: The Murals - Including Digital Restoration Photographs ....... 25

    *Pueblo Corn Dancers.*
        Alfonso Roybal, Awa Tsireh (1895–1955): ............................................. 26

    *Blueface Navajo Yeibichai Dancers.*
        Harrison Begay, Haashké yah Niyá (The Wandering Boy), (1914–2012): ... 28

    *Apache Mountain Spirit Dancer.*
        Ignatius Palmer (1922–1985): .................................................................. 29

    *Apache Mountain Spirit Dancer.*
        Wilson Dewey (1915–1969): .................................................................... 30

    *Straight Beaked Bird and Curved Beak Bird*
        Tony Martinez, Popovi Da (Red Fox), (1922–1971): .............................. 31

*Cochiti Butterfly Dancers.*
   Joe H. Herrera, See Ru (Blue Bird), (1923–2001): ..................................................................32

*Pueblo Family Gathering Corn.*
   Olive Rush (1873-1966) ............................................................................................................33

*Navajo Women on Horseback*
   Olive Rush (1873-1966): ..........................................................................................................34

*Santa Clara Women Selling Pottery.*
   Pablita Velarde, Tse Twan (Golden Dawn), (1918–2006): .....................................................35

*Animals in a Forest.*
   Merina Lujan Hopkins, Pop Chalee (Blue Flower), (1906–1993): .........................................36

*Pueblo Deer Dancers*
   Olive Rush (1873-1966): ..........................................................................................................37

*Butterfly Maiden*
   Tony Martinez, Popovi Da (Red Fox), (1922–1971):
*Cochiti Woman Deer Dancer.*
   Joe H. Herrera, See Ru (Blue Bird), (1923–2001): ..................................................................38

*Deer Dancer.*
   Ben Quintana, Há-ā- tee, (1923–1944):
*Corn Dancer.*
   Theodore Suina, Ku-Pe-Ru (Snow), (1918–aft. 2018?): ..........................................................39

*Navajo Ceremonial Antelope Hunt.*
   Narciso Platero Abeyta, Ha So Deh, (1918-1998) ...................................................................40

**References** .........................................................................................................................................42

**Appendix A: Maisel Murals Artist Overview Table** ......................................................................45
**Appendix B: Technical Data Concerning the Photographs** ..........................................................46
**Appendix C: Santa Clara Pueblo in 1940** .......................................................................................47

**List of Figures for Chapters One Through Nine**
   **Figure 1:** Maisel's Entrance in 2011................................................................................5
   **Figure 2:** Maisel's Postcard, 1940 ...................................................................................6
   **Figure 3:** Before and After Images of *Cochiti Woman Deer Dancer* by Joe Herrera............................6

**Figure 4:** Detail of Maisel Paintings from the 1940 Postcard ..................................................... 7
**Figure 5:** Santa Fe Indian School *The Studio* Classroom ca. 1940 ............................................. 8
**Figure 6:** Snapshots Made by Maria Chabot as the Murals Were being Painted ......................... 10
**Figure 7:** Detail of a Wedding Vase, Velarde's Painting; Photograph of Similar by Legoria Tefoya. 16
**Figure 8:** Detail of Feet from Awa Tsireh's Painting - Detail .................................................... 17
**Figure 9:** Detail of Feet from Awa Tsireh's Painting - Movement ............................................. 19
**Figure 10:** Detail of Abeyta's *Navajo Ceremonial Antelope Hunt* Showing a Male and a Female ....... 19
**Figure 11:** Sacred Clown, Called a *Kossa* by the Tewa, from Awa Tsireh's Painting ..................... 20
**Figure 12:** A Self-portrait Detail from Pablita Velarde's Painting and a Photograph of Her ............. 22
**Figure 13:** The Maisel's Murals Layout ................................................................................. 23

# ACKNOWLEDGMENTS

To Jennifer Coile for her critical reading of the text; expert proof reading and all around encouragement.

To John Robrock, an excellent art teacher and observer for his comments on technical aspects of the murals.

To Joe Mildenberger, an animation artist of considerable skill and accomplishment for his assistance with the digital restorations.

To Sascha T. Scott, PhD, art historian at Syracuse University in New York and a specialist in Southwestern art for her comments, encouragement and insightful publications.

To Gordon Bronitsky, PhD, a professional in the world of Native American arts, for his insights into indigenous cultures, as well as his excellent proofing skills and commentary.

To my wife Marcia for never letting thoughts of Maisel's stray from my mind.

# FOREWARD

My wish is that increased awareness and understanding of the Maisel's Murals will lead to their further recognition as unique treasures of Southwestern Native American art. The current owners of Maisel's store, and hence the Murals, have a long history of community involvement, a most encouraging sign for the mural's stewardship and public access.

In an ideal future scenario, the condition of the Murals would be professionally evaluated followed by implementing recommendations for their cleaning and restoration.

Opportunities for educational and celebratory activities abound, such as a local and traveling exhibitions of the Murals, along the lines of the shows Olive Rush organized and produced for the Santa Fe Indian School (SFIS) under the auspices of the Works Progress Administration (WPA) in the 1930s and developing curriculum materials for young people. The photographs taken by the Albuquerque Historical Society (HAI) in 2020 and donated to the Albuquerque Museum of History and Art may be of the quality suitable for potential future projects.

This book is not an academic work, and hence is written in the first person without footnotes. However, a list of references is included and the 2018 book has an extensive listing of references.

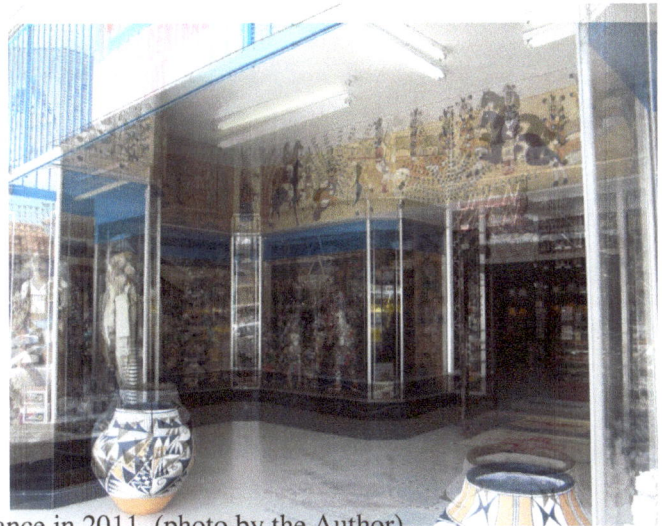

Figure 1: Maisel's entrance in 2011. (photo by the Author)

## INTRODUCTION

This book is a follow-on to *The Maisel's Murals 1939 - Native American Art of the American Southwest* published by Sunstone Press, Santa Fe, New Mexico in 2018. However, it is a stand-alone publication designed to be a viewer guide to the subject art works, i.e. a companion for the observer to assist in the understanding of what they are seeing when they look at the murals and to allow for individual interpretation of what is being viewed, rather than just be a presentation of names, date, and basic facts about the murals. For that information, the reader is referred to the aforementioned book. However, two items have been updated and are provided in this book to give the reader an appropriate level of contextual background: (1) "Table 1: Maisel's Murals Artist Overview," in Appendix A, and (2) "Figure 1: Maisel's Murals Layout," with the newly restored images, in Chapter Seven, "A Unified Design Concept, pg. 23.

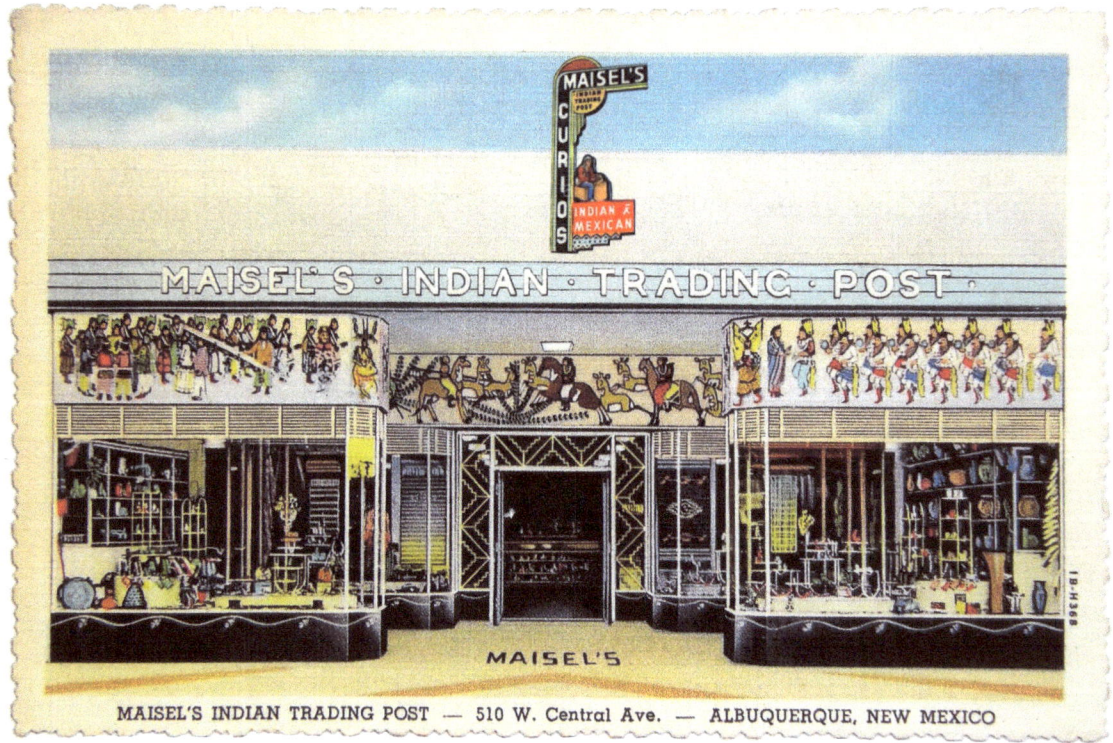

**Figure 2:** Maisel's Postcard, 1940. (Author's collection)

# CHAPTER ONE:
# HOW THIS BOOK CAME ABOUT

The 2018 book did not achieve all of the goals that I had wished for in presenting the murals. It was put into publication fairly quickly as it became apparent the ownership of the Maisel store and its use was going to pass from the Maisel family to a new owner. This indeed transpired the year of publication and the Maisel's store was permanently closed by the late summer of 2019. To no surprise the entry vestibules of the store, where most of the murals are located, are shuttered and have remained so throughout 2020.

I was first attracted to the murals as an undergraduate at the University of New Mexico some fifty years ago. The idea for a book on the murals initially coalesced in about 2012 after moving back to Albuquerque, after retiring from a career in southern California. However, I was delayed by other projects and ongoing research, the need for high quality photographs and a desire to form a collaboration with an art historian familiar with Southwestern Native American art.

While well received, the 2018 publication did not immediately engender the level of interest and enthusiasm that I hoped. Then, in the late summer of 2020 I was approached by a producer for a local Public Broadcasting Station show on New Mexico Arts, ¡Colores!. This producer had observed members of the HAI taking photographs of the murals and my name was suggested as someone who knew something about them. The resulting short video was posted online on September 10, 2020 and continues to generate viewership. One immediate result of which was my being asked to give a virtual lecture on the murals for the HAI.

Reviewing past research, and undertaking new research on the murals, in preparation for the video interview and subsequent lecture, opened up considerably expanded perspectives on the murals. The extent of new information and insights quickly transmogrified into the need for a new work on the murals. So now there are two books, and while each is a complete work unto itself, together they fulfill my vision of a comprehensive Maisel's Murals overview from some years ago.

## CHAPTER TWO:
## VIRTUAL RESTORATION

A turning point in reassessing the murals came from seeing images with enhanced contrast, i.e. the HAI images taken in 2020, used in the PBS video. The noticeable increased color saturation and contrast led me to conclude that such images would bring an clearer view of the murals and that republication of them might be in order. However, the high resolution unmodified versions of the HAI images were donated to the Albuquerque Museum of History and Art, and they couldn't be accessed for public use without the Museum's approval prior to publication, including licensing and use fees, along with a formal user agreement. I knew this would require time and money to obtain.

Fortunately, I already had images at the requisite image quality, taken between 2015 and 2017 in anticipation of the initial Maisel's book (see Appendix B.) It is these images that are the basis of those used in this book. But without HAI's interest in recordation of the murals, these prior images would most likely have continued to remain neglected in my files.

With those images at hand, the process of digital restoration could be explored. Digital restoration and reconstruction has in recent years become an important tool for archaeology and by extension tourism. Digital techniques are especially applicable to architecture, given that most architectural drawing in recent years is done on a computer. For example there is a wonderful virtual reconstruction of the Northwest Palace at Nimrud, Assyria and a tourist with a virtual reality headset can walk the streets of ancient Pompeii or view the murals on the walls of Nero's Palace, the Domus Aurea, in Rome. The Leonardo Da Vinci painting of "the Last Supper" can now be viewed as a close approximation of the original and medieval murals have been brought back to their former glory - and all without physically touching the original. A central precept of restoration, as with medicine, "do no harm" can now be fully realized.

Native American art of the first half of the 20th century is especially well suited to digital restoration. These paintings generally have a monochromatic background and flaws to the painting surface, e.g. cracks in the plaster are easily removed. I was astounded at how successful relatively minimal touch-up was able to bring the Maisel's Murals back to life after 80 years of street grime, and the effects of smoke and water damage from a fire in the 1970s. While not a professional in the field of restoration, I have used the Photoshop graphics program in a professional capacity for fifteen years. I have directed a number of historic resource evaluations, including literally hundreds

- 4 -

of 20th century postal facilities in the Western United States, many of which contain murals of a comparable age to those at Maisel's. Perhaps most importantly, my good friend artist Joe Mildenberger, currently an animation supervisor for Warner Brothers in Los Angeles, has offered his help and advise.

Some viewers may be somewhat put-off by images in this book since they are accustomed to seeing the murals a certain way. In our culture old is often associated with good, and dirt and grime on an object's surface becomes viewed as a desirable patina. The physical alteration of cleaning a surface can engender strong opinions; think of the cleaning of the Sistine Chapel ceiling some years ago. But with a digital restoration, there is no physical impact on the original. The key issue affecting the original murals appears to be soot from the fire, and the washing away of some paint, but the fading is not significant, nor is change in colors due to the aging of materials. Despite some cracking, the plaster surface is essentially intact.

The ultimate goal of this book is to help "see" the murals as they were meant to be seen. I found the process of digital cleaning and repairing them highly rewarding. By looking in detail, by spending a day or more on each mural, and by weighing subjective decisions on background color and brightness/contrast of some aspect of a painting, I gained a new understanding and appreciation of the murals. This process alone was well worth the effort.

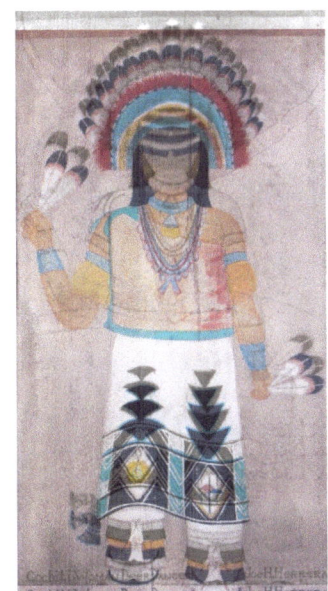 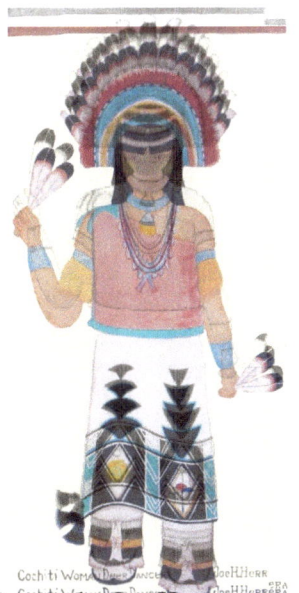

**Figure 3:** Before and After Images of *Cochiti Woman Deer Dancer* by Joe Herrera.

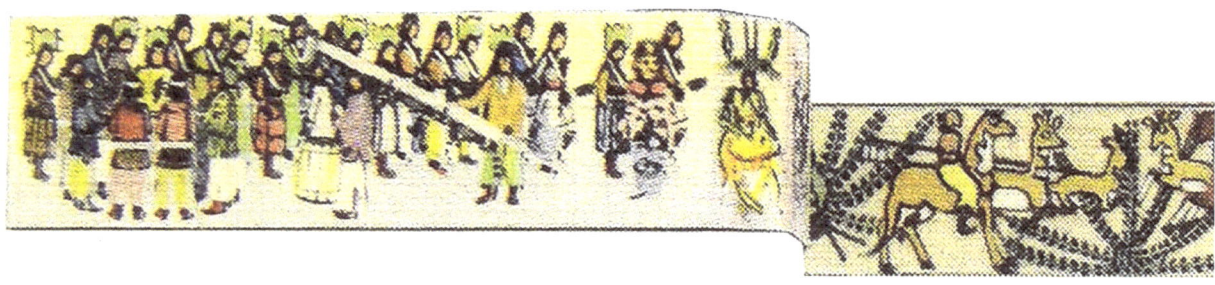

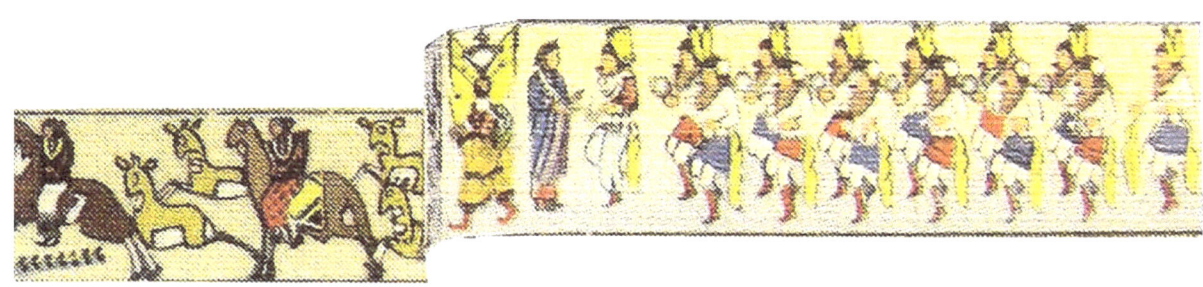

**Figure 4:** Detail of Maisel paintings from the 1940 postcard of the Maisel's store shown as Figure 2. It is a linen postcard based on a black and white photograph that has been retouched by hand and printed using a four-color halftone process. The result is a color image that has a greater color saturation than a natural scene and possible airbrushed details not found in the original photograph.

Despite the manipulation and printing limitations of the postcard it proved highly instructive when working on the digital restorations. The colors are clearly a bit "off" but there is a good indication of the overall look of the murals when freshly painted. The flat monochrome background is very clear, as is the fact that the murals on the street frontage had a two color background, while the *Navajo Ceremonial Antelope Hunt* at the rear has a single color background.

# CHAPTER THREE:
## *THE STUDIO* STYLE

An introduction to Native American art in the 1930s, along with general background on Dorothy Dunn and SFIS art program, whom most of the Maisel artists studied under, is found in the 2018 book on Maisel's Murals and will not be repeated here. The following supplements that prior discussion.

The Pueblo artists during the first decades of the 20th century were strongly encouraged by anthropologists, a number of whom were important figures in Santa Fe, to depict scenes of Pueblo life. Anthropologist Edgar J. Hewett in 1917 commissioned Crescencio Martinez of San Ildefonso Pueblo to paint a series of images, many on pottery tiles, of public ceremonial dances. The Martinez paintings, while not the earliest Pueblo paintings targeted for the Anglo community, can be seen as the start of the Pueblo art movement, later formalized as *The Studio* style.

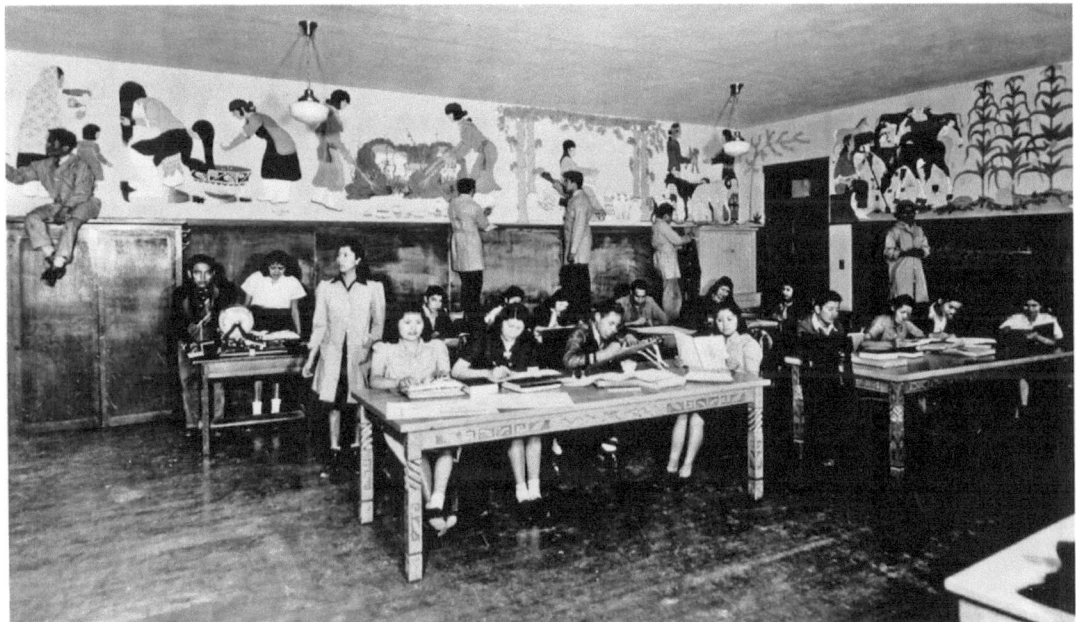

**Figure 5:** Santa Fe Indian School *The Studio* classroom ca. 1940, photo by Ernest Knee. The 1932 murals surrounding the classroom interior were destroyed in 2008. (MNM 030934)

# CHAPTER FOUR:
# THE ARTISTS

The eleven Native American artists (see Appendix A) who worked on the Maisel's Murals ranged in age from forty-four year old Awa Tsireh, to three sixteen year olds: See Ru (Joe Herrera), Popovi Da (Tony Martinez) and Ha-A-Tee (Ben Quintana.) Seven of the artists had been students at the Santa Fe Indian School (SFIS) art program called *The Studio* and had studied under its founder Dorothy Dunn, as well as having received instruction in mural painting by Olive Rush, who served as an adjunct instructor. The youngest three artists, while *The Studio* students, would have had limited instruction under Dunn, who left the SFIS in 1937. These three received most of their art instruction under Geronima Cruz Montoya who took over *The Studio* program following Dunn's departure. Thus only one Native American artist who did not study at *The Studio* was Awa Tsireh, who was too old to have studied there.

The table shows that all but one male artist served in World War II, which started not long after the Maisel's Murals project. Ben Quintana, one of the most promising artists of his time, died in battle in the South Pacific at the age of twenty-three and was posthumously awarded a Silver Star. He was one of the famous Navajo codetalkers.

Most of the Native American artists who worked on the Maisel project became well known in subsequent decades with their works found in various museum collections in New Mexico and throughout the United States, as well as in some international collections.

Olive Rush, who directed the Maisel project, was sixty years old in 1939, and this was to be the last of her many mural projects with Native Americans. Several of the Maisel's Murals painters had participated in travelling mural shows she organized during the 1930s, as well as having had worked with her on WPA sponsored mural projects throughout the country that she had coordinated.

The artists who painted the Maisel's Murals are:

## Narciso Platero Abeyta, Ha So Deh, (1918–1998):
*Navajo Antelope Hunt.*
Narciso Abeyta was a Navajo born at Correo, New Mexico on the Tohajiilee Navajo Reservation. He did not follow the tradition of the earlier Southwestern artists but instead modeled his work after commercial and contemporary realist European artists.

## Harrison Begay, Haashké yah Nívá (The Wandering Boy), (1914–2012):
*Blueface Navajo Yeibichai Dancers.*
Harrison Begay was a Navajo born at Whitecone near Greasewood Springs, Arizona. He was interested in art as a child, and began his formal art education at the Santa Fe Indian School under Dorothy Dunn between 1934 and 1939.

## Wilson Dewey, (1915–1969):
*Apache Mountain Spirit Dancer.*
Wilson Dewey was a San Carlos Apache and nephew of Maria Martinez, the San Ildefonso potter. He was a student at the Santa Fe Indian School for three years beginning in 1935 and finishing his final year of education at the Albuquerque Indian School in 1941.

## Joe H. Herrera, See Ru (Blue Bird), (1923–2001):
*Cochiti Deer Dancer* and *Butterfly Dancers*.
Joe Herrera was born at Cochiti Pueblo in 1921, his father's home. His mother was the famous painter Tonita Pena from San Ildefonso Pueblo, and she was his first teacher.

## Merina Lujan Hopkins, Pop Chalee (Blue Flower), (1906–1993):
*Forest Scene.*
Chalee was born in Castle Gate, Utah to a Taos Pueblo father from the well-known Lujan family (her uncle was Tony Lujan, husband of Mabel Dodge) and an East Indian/Swiss mother. She studied art under Dorothy Dunn at *The Studio* from 1935 to 1937, having been given special dispensation because she was too old for the art school program.

**Tony Martinez, Popovi Da (Red Fox), (1922–1971):**
*Curved* and *Straight Billed Bird,* and *Butterfly Maiden*.
Popovi Da was born at San Ildefonso Pueblo, the son of famous San Ildefonso potter Maria Martinez and her artist husband Julian Martinez. He was educated at the Santa Fe Indian School, where he graduated in 1939 at the age of sixteen.

**Ignatius Palmer (1922–1985):**
*Apache Mountain Spirit Dancer.*
Palmer was a Chiricahua Apache from the Mescalero Apache Reservation.

**Ben Quintana, Há-ā- tee, (1923–1944):**
*Chchiti Deer Dancer.*
Quintana was born at Cochiti Pueblo. He attended the pueblo school, where he painted his first mural while in the fifth grade.

**Alfonso Roybal, Awa Tsireh (1895–1955):**
*Pueblo Corn Dancers.*
Awa Tsireh of San Ildefonso Pueblo was one of the first of the "modern" Pueblo artists. He almost gave up art when his copies of kiva frescoes angered the San Ildefonso elders and he was severely punished.

**Theodore Suina, Ku-Pe-Ru (Snow), (1918–aft. 2018?):**
*Cochiti Corn Dances.*
Ku-Pe-Ru was born at Cochiti Pueblo. In 1938, he enrolled at the Indian School in Santa Fe and studied art, graduating in 1942.

**Pablita Velarde, Tse Twan (Golden Dawn), (1918–2006):** *Santa Clara Women Selling Pottery.*
Pablita was from Santa Clara Pueblo. In 1932 she became a student at the Santa Fe Indian School art program.

# CHAPTER FIVE:
# PAINTING THE MURALS

Olive Rush purchased the materials used by the artists and hired professional plasterers to prepare the painting surface. The paints were high quality casein tempera which uses curdled milk as the protein binder.

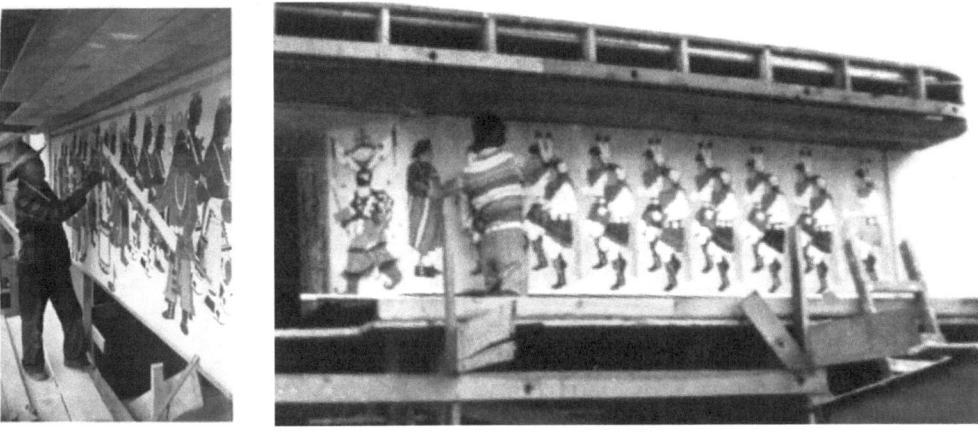

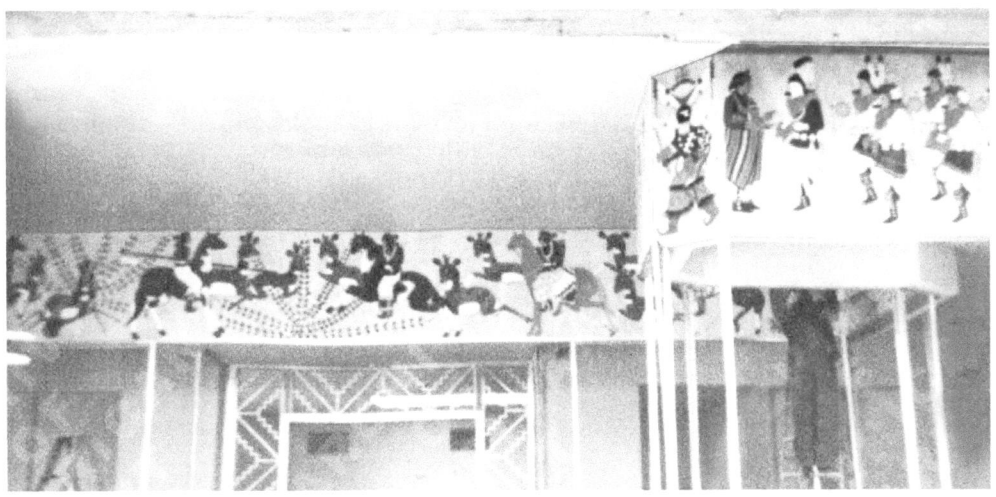

**Figure 6:** Snapshots made by Maria Chabot as the murals were being painted. (Olive Rush Papers, 1879 1967, Archives of American Art, Smithsonian Institution.)

# CHAPTER: SIX
# OVERALL CONSIDERATIONS

Before looking at the Maisel's Murals individually, there are several key concepts for the viewer to keep in mind. These general concepts are applicable to other paintings of the same genre, but are especially relevant to the subject at hand. A number of them appear to be dichotomies, e.g. the paintings are overly simplified, yet stunningly detailed, and the images are static, yet show considerable movement. Such aspects of the art should be seen as ends of a continuum, rather than either/or.

All of the Maisel's Murals share several common characteristics informed by the artistic style formalized by Dorothy Bunn. J. J. Brody describes *The Studio* style in his 1971 book *Indian Painters and White Patrons* as being the sole creation of Bunn. Bunn had what we would see today as a paternalistic view of Native Americans. What she saw first were rapidly disappearing cultures that needed preservation, and that Native Americans had a innate artistic talents that needed to be developed and promoted. The result was a narrow view of Native Americans who should restrict their artistic expression to the confines of their own specific cultural affiliation. Her views on art and goals are described in detail in her 1968 book *American Indian Painting of the Southwest and Plains Area*.

Dunn drew heavily on the work of the first generation of Native American painters from the late 19th and early 20th centuries. These artists include Albert Looking Elk and Ben Lujan from Taos Pueblo; Julian Martinez, Crescenco Martinez, Tonita Pena and Awa Tsireh from San Ildefonso Pueblo; and Naiche a Chiricahua Apache. These artists are typically described as untrained, but this is true only in a European sense.

The work of this initial grouping of artists was primarily influenced by their own cultural affiliations. For the Puebloans this includes Kiva (ceremonial chamber) art, an ancient and highly developed painting process, pictographs/petroglyphs, pottery painting and textile designs. The Dine (Navajo) have a highly refined tradition of sandpainting. All of these influence go back to the first inhabitants of North America.

- 12 -

# 1: Characteristics Common to All the Murals

These characteristics include:

(a) A flat plain, generally monochromatic, background.
(b) Images and figures lack European three-point perspective. Perspective is rather implied by size relationship and view orientation.
(c) figures and objects are outlined to enhance their visibility.

# 2: First and Second Generation Artists

Only Awa Tsireh was a member of the so-called "first generation" of Southwestern Native artists, although several of the artists, including the three youngest ones, painted in this earliest style. Others, such as Pop Chalee had a unique iconoclast presentation and Narciso Abeyta's work is strongly influenced by contemporary commercial and realist European Art. Following his service in WWII, he studied under modernist painter Raymond Johnson at the University of New Mexico.

The other artists fall somewhere in a range of stylistic conventions. In looking at the murals as a whole, the two murals on the Central Avenue street frontage, *Pueblo Corn Dancers* by Awa Tsireh to the east and *Navajo Yeibichai* to the west are the most characteristic of the earliest style of formal Southwestern Painting that was directly influencing Dorothy Dunn's *The Studio* style. The long mural *Navajo Ceremonial Antelope Hunt* by Narcisco Plater Abeyta is the mural most closely related to contemporary styles of the late 1930s.

The three compositions by Olive Rush, who was not Native American and had considerable European art training, along with the study of Persian and Asian arts fits into a category of her own. While at first glance her Maisel's work looks like something out of *The Studio* this is only true because of the subject matter and monochrome background. Her paintings reflect a broad range of European and Asian influences, and include very non-Southwestern design/form references as well as showing perspective conventions that come from of European and Asian influences.

# 3: Creativity Through Constraint

Dorothy Dunn would most likely have agreed with Adam Richardson's 2013 essay *Boosting Creativity Through Constraints*, paraphrased and selectively modified in part as follows:

Conventional wisdom holds that the best way to boost creativity is to be unshackled from constraints. The less you have to worry about, the more open to individual ideas, the theory goes. Yet constraints have a Goldilocks quality: too many and you will suffocate in stale

> *thinking, too few and you risk a rambling vision quest (which may in fact be your purpose as an artist.) The key to spurring creativity isn't the removal of all constraints. Ideally you should impose only those constraints that move you toward clarity of purpose.*

Or as Igor Stravinsky said:

> *...my freedom will be so much the greater and more meaningful the more narrowly I limit my field of action and the more I surround myself with obstacles. Whatever diminishes constraint, diminishes strength. The more constraints one imposes, the more one frees one's self of the chains that shackle the spirit.*

A number of *The Studio* students later chafed under the restrictions imposed upon them and broke out into new and more expansive forms and different media.

## 4. Precision and Detail

The detail presented in the earliest Maisel's paintings, and that of sixteen year old Ben Quintana, is truly stunning. I was surprised at the precision of execution found in the representational scenes. This is not the case with most examples of later *Studio* style following their gross commercialization, especially into the second half of the 20th century and which is continuing to this day. This is likely a reflection of art movements in general which tend to degrade following excessive commercialization and the rise of new movements that look to the new and fresh and reject what had come before.

The precision of the earlier works should be no surprise. Native American rituals are serious affairs. The Pueblos, with whom I am most familiar, are compulsively fixated on "getting it right." There is no room for mistakes because the rituals inform how various aspects of the world works, and the perceived consequences of getting something wrong are potentially harmful. For instance if something falls off or comes loose from a dancer's regalia during a ceremonial dance, there are attendants who immediately fix the issue. While not available for outsiders to see (see **6. Resistance** below) there is no question that Kiva paintings, which have great sacred significance must be accurate. Painters of Awa Tsireh's time reflect this accuracy of execution in their painting. It would have been second nature to persons of their generation.

This is not to say that such accuracy is restricted to only the earliest progenitors of the subject movement. The artist Ben Quintana's manages to show nuanced detail of the subject's regalia and imply detail and depth on a flat surface within the confines of the style, see "**8. Kitsch - When Art**

**Become Banal."** However, it was under the tutorship of Dorothy Dunn and Olive Rush that they learned fundamentals of artistic expression. For many, their reaction to - and breaking away from - *The Studio* lead to the richness and variety of expression found today in Native American arts.

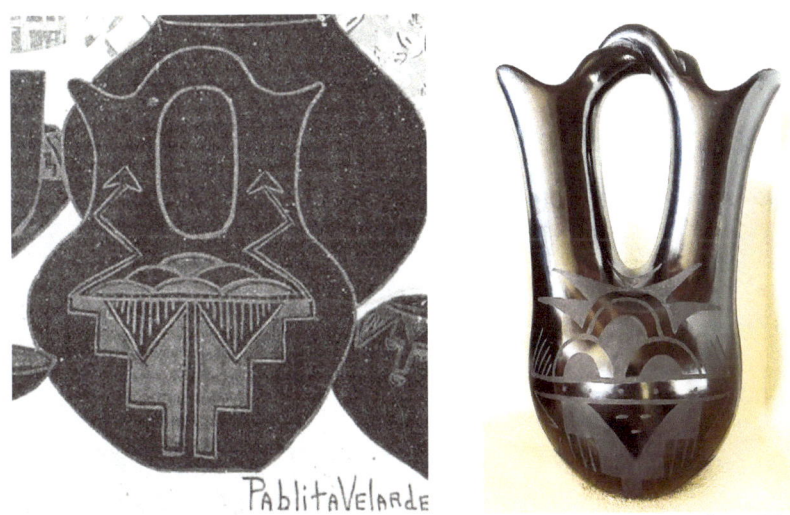

**Figure 7:** Detail of a Wedding Vase from Pablita Velarde's painting of *Santa Clara Women Selling Pottery* on the left and a photograph of a strikingly similar Wedding Vase made by Legoria Tefoya, Pablita's sister. The arrow tipped lighting bolts pointing up on the painted vase are also found, but not visible in this photo, pointing down on the actual vase. (l. detail from a black and white image of Velarde's painting found in Dunn: 1968; r. signed vase in the Author's collection.)

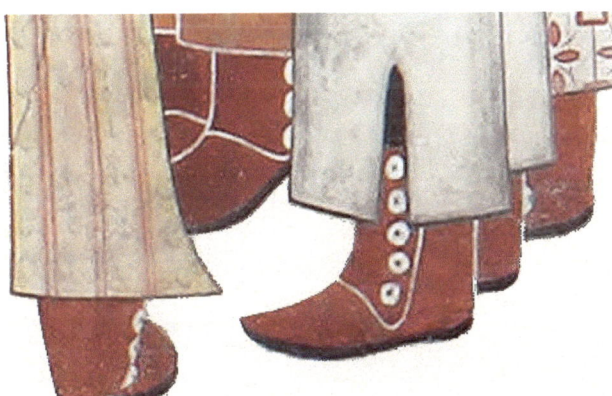

**Figure 8:** Detail of feet from Awa Tsireh's painting of a *Pueblo Corn Dance*. Note the overlap of the leather, black dyed soles, and the silver buttons seen full on and indicated in profile.

## 5: Movement

With a lack of three-point perspective being a hallmark of the art considered here, the artist incorporates other techniques to show movement. Clear examples of this are seen in the differing depictions of *Apache Mountain Spirit Dancers*, and the *Pueblo Corn Dancers* contrasted with the *Navajo Yeibichi Dancers*. In both cases, movement is indicated by a raised foot. A related techniques is to show one hand raised and one lowered, or a bent torso.

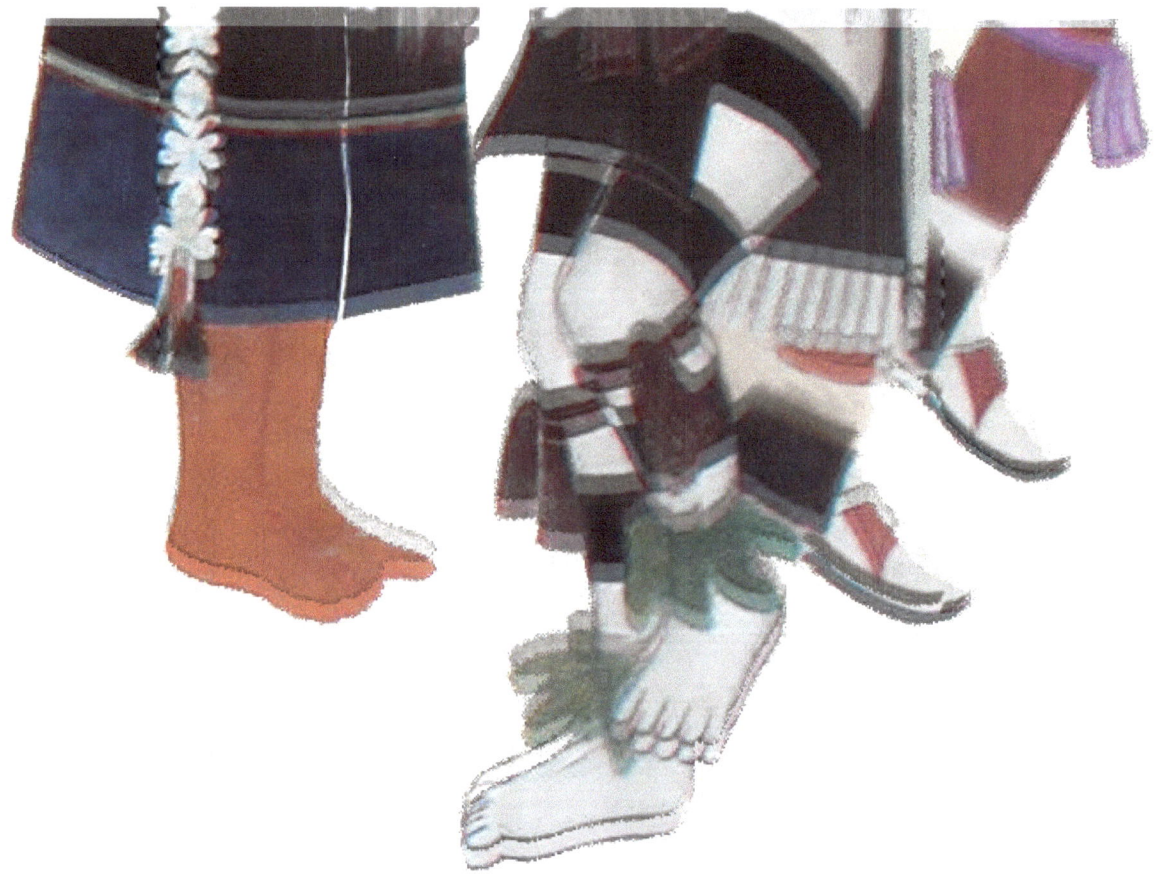

**Figure 9:** Here is another detail of feet from Awa Tsireh's painting of a *Pueblo Corn Dance*. Movement is indicated by the relative position of the feet, with the woman standing, the *Kossa* sacred clown stomping and the male dancer executing the shuffle step of the dance.

## 6: Men and Women

Only two of the eleven Native American artists who worked on the Maisel's Murals were women, which is not surprising given that painting was seen as men's work. Women were potters. But of course the entire project was supervised by a woman, Olive Rush.

Of the seventy figures depicted in the murals twenty-five are women and forty-five are men. Both men and women are represented in ceremonial as well as domestic scenes.

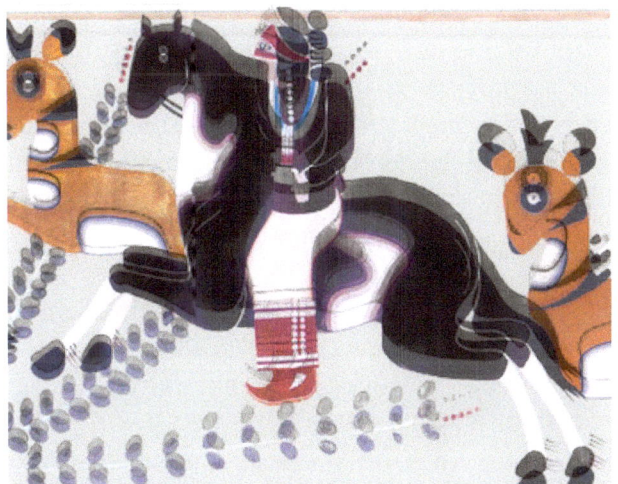 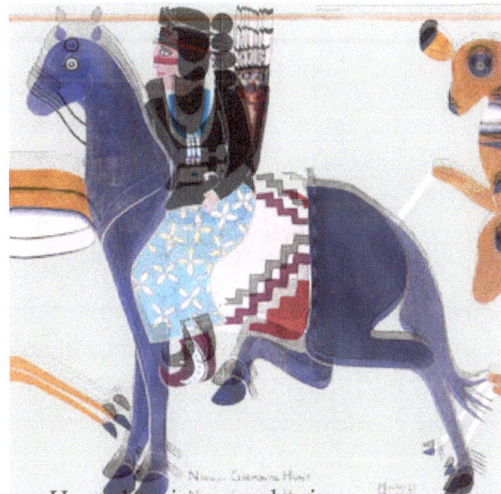

**Figure 10:** Detail of Abeyta's *Navajo Ceremonial Antelope Hunt* showing a male rider on the left and a female rider to the right.

## 7: Resistance

Some of the first generation of Pueblo artists had worked on archaeological projects conducted by Edgar Hewett on the Parjarito Palateau west of Santa Fe. This put the Native American workers in a real bind. Here were paying jobs when employment was scarce, but on the other hand they were disturbing graves, sacred spaces, and, what for them were still living villages, although no longer inhabited by living persons. And then came pressure, initially by the anthropological community and tourists who want something "authentic," to express aspects of Pueblo life through paintings. This conundrum is addressed by art historian Sascha T. Scott's 2020 paper *Ana-Ethnographic Representation: Early Modern Pueblo Painters, Scientific Colonialism, and Tactics of Refusal*.

The result is that the Native Americans were and are now highly selective in what they choose to represent. Scott coined the term "ana-ethnographic" to describe how Native American artists gave the mostly Anglo colonizers what they wanted while still being able to "honor and celebrate ideas fundamental to Pueblo life and have potent meaning for the makers and their communities." This is very much to be case with the Maisel's Murals.

Many indigenous peoples, and certainly Indigenous cultures of the Southwest, view knowledge as power in the sense that there are aspects of community life, in particular those expressed by ceremonialism, that must be closely guarded. Such knowledge is not only powerful, but also very dangerous. Secrecy is important to protect potentially dangerous knowledge and should therefore not be shared, known only to those with the proper training to deal with it.

Asking a direct question about a ceremonial dance is considered quite rude and highly improper for any viewer of a public ceremonial dance. This could revel dangerous sacred information meant only for the initiated. It may also by extension be embarrassing to the person being asked, who most probably does not know the full answer.

The Pueblo view that some knowledge must be kept secret and not shared at first might seem to be the antithesis of a Western, in particular academic, view with the idea that all knowledge should be shared. This is, after all, a basic tenant of scientific inquiry. However, this is not universally the case. There is knowledge which Western cultures carefully guard and is shared only with those who have been properly "initiated" as having a reason to know. Military weapons and industrial process information, often of a scientific nature, fall into this category. The nuclear codes are closely guarded, for such knowledge if wide spread would be very dangerous.

When looking at the Maisel's Murals you are seeing only the select aspects of Native American culture that the artist wants to share. This is a limited view and parts may have been left out or altered to show only what you are meant to see. It should be noted that what to show and what not to show was a dilemma that the artists struggled with. Both Awa Tsireh and Pablita Velarde were, strongly criticized by Pueblo leaders for what they depicted in some of their paintings. As a young man Awa Tsireh was severely beaten for his transgression in painting kiva images.

## 8. Engaging the Viewer

Typically in a *The Studio* style painting the viewer is a detached observer of a Native American tableau. However there are exceptions, two of which are quite prominent in the Maisel's Murals. If a figure is engaging a viewer in such paintings, there will be a reason, as is apparent in the examples described below.

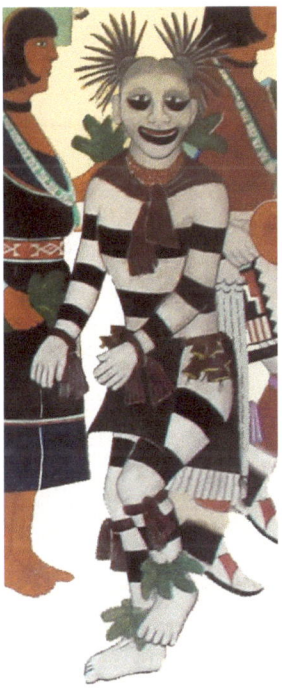

**Figure 11:** This sacred clown, called a *Kossa* by the Tewa, is at the far right of Awa Tsireh's painting *Pueblo Corn Dancers*. This is a very powerful figure and not to be trifled with. He is an enforcer and will make fun of just about anyone who catches his eye, e.g. talking and not paying attention during a dance, not dressing appropriately or not following the rules such as trying to sneak a photograph. Tourists are a typical target. *Kossa* are said to be able to speak any language and are prone to rude jokes and sexual inuendo. This *Kossa* is looking straight at the viewer, and any Pueblo person would immediately realize that this is attention you would rather not have. Given that most of the viewers of the Maisel's Murals will be Anglo "tourists", painting the *Kossa* as he has here is an inside joke, see subsection **7. Resistance**.

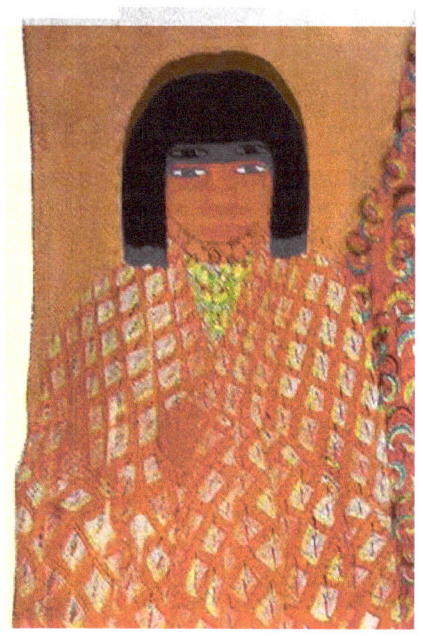 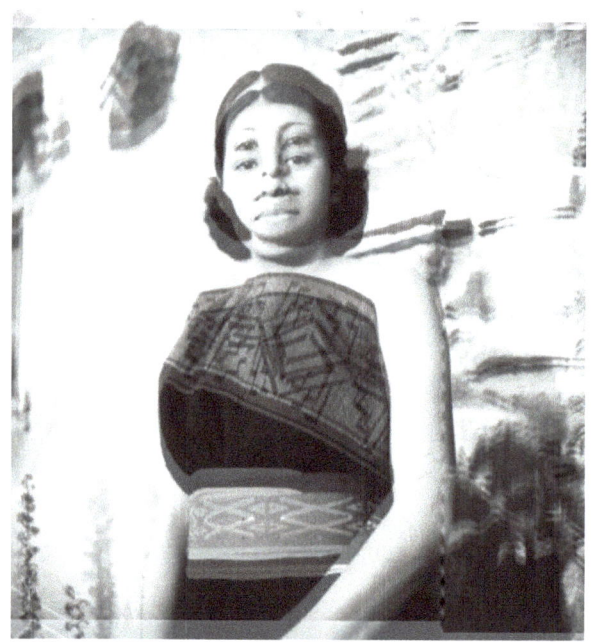

Figure 13: A detail from Pablita Velarde's painting *Santa Clara Women Selling Pottery* and a photograph of Velarde taken at Seton Village, the home / school / workshop of her friend, artist Ernest Thompson Seton taken just a few months prior to the Maisel's Murals. There is no documentary evidence that this is a self-portrait, however Velarde is known to have occasionally inserted herself in her paintings, as well as being quite forthright and having something of a mischievous nature. The painting depicts Velarde with a typical woman's hair style with long bangs, while the photograph shows her with a contemporary Anglo hairstyle (photograph by Harold Kellogg, dated 1938; Museum of New Mexico, Negative Number 07754.)

## 9. Kitsch - When Art Becomes Banal

There is considerable literature on addressing kitsch. Tomáš Kulka, in *Kitsch and Art*, states that kitsch "has an undeniable mass-appeal" and is "considered (by the art-educated elite) bad", and that it has three essential conditions:
 a. Kitsch depicts a beautiful or highly emotionally charged subject;
 b. The depicted subject is instantly and effortlessly identifiable;
 c. Kitsch does not substantially enrich our associations related to the depicted subject.

The Austrian writer Hermann Broch states that the essence of kitsch is imitation, in that kitsch mimics its immediate predecessor intending to "copy the beautiful, not the good." While German critic Walther Benjamin posits that kitsch, "offers instantaneous emotional gratification without intellectual effort":

This is without question what happened to *The Studio* style and for which it has been much criticized, including the art works by Native American artists such as painter R. C. Gorman and sculptor Allen Houser, the later a student at *The Studio* program. While each of these artists maintained artistic integrity in their own work, there is no little irony the magnitude of kitsch reproduction copies of their art, and crass commercialism from mugs to T-towels.

However, when it comes to the Maisel's Murals, that are clearly meant to inform and have many layers of meaning not immediately apparent to the casual viewer, kitsch clearly does not apply.

# CHAPTER SEVEN:
# A UNIFIED DESIGN CONCEPT

The Maisel's Murals, with each mural being a fully formed painting in its own right, are part of an overall design construct. Unfortunately, no documentation has ever been found that describes the overriding conception of the murals. Olive Rush, despite leaving a plethora of documents and interviews never directly discussed her work on Marisel's in print, nor did any of the artists who worked on the project describe the paintings or their working together on the Murals.

Olive Rush, perhaps in consultation with Geronima Cruz Montoya, the director of the SFIS art program at the time, selected the artists she wanted to work on the Maisel project. She clearly wanted the murals to represent a range of artists including young promising students, artists who had established themselves, as well as artists who would represent the first generation of the Southwestern Native American art movement.

How much Rush directed the subject matter of the paintings is not clear. The murals were clearly not meant to be exploratory or experimental, but rather intended to highlight the best work of each individual. The themes presented in the murals were ones that the various artist were well familiar with and had previously painted.

The Murals were apparently a collaboration between the artists and Rush, with Rush guiding the overall presentation. All but the expansive *Navajo Ceremonial Antelope Hunt* along the south wall above the front doors are opposite pairs. This pairing starts with the street frontage large groups of dancers with *Pueblo Corn Dances* to the east and *Navajo Yeibichai Dancers* to the west. As one moves toward the front entrance doors, there are a series of opposed related images: Apache Dancers; two late summer/fall scenes, a Butterfly Dance across from a Pueblo family gathering corn; two single female dancers; two everyday life scenes, one Navajo, one Pueblo; two geometric bird designs; two forest scenes; and two Cochiti women dancers. In addition three of the pairs contrast a summer dance with a winter dance. and two pairs contrast female dancers in profile with female dancers in a frontal view. There is also a diagonal pairing of a Cochiti Women Deer dancers, one in profile and one face on.

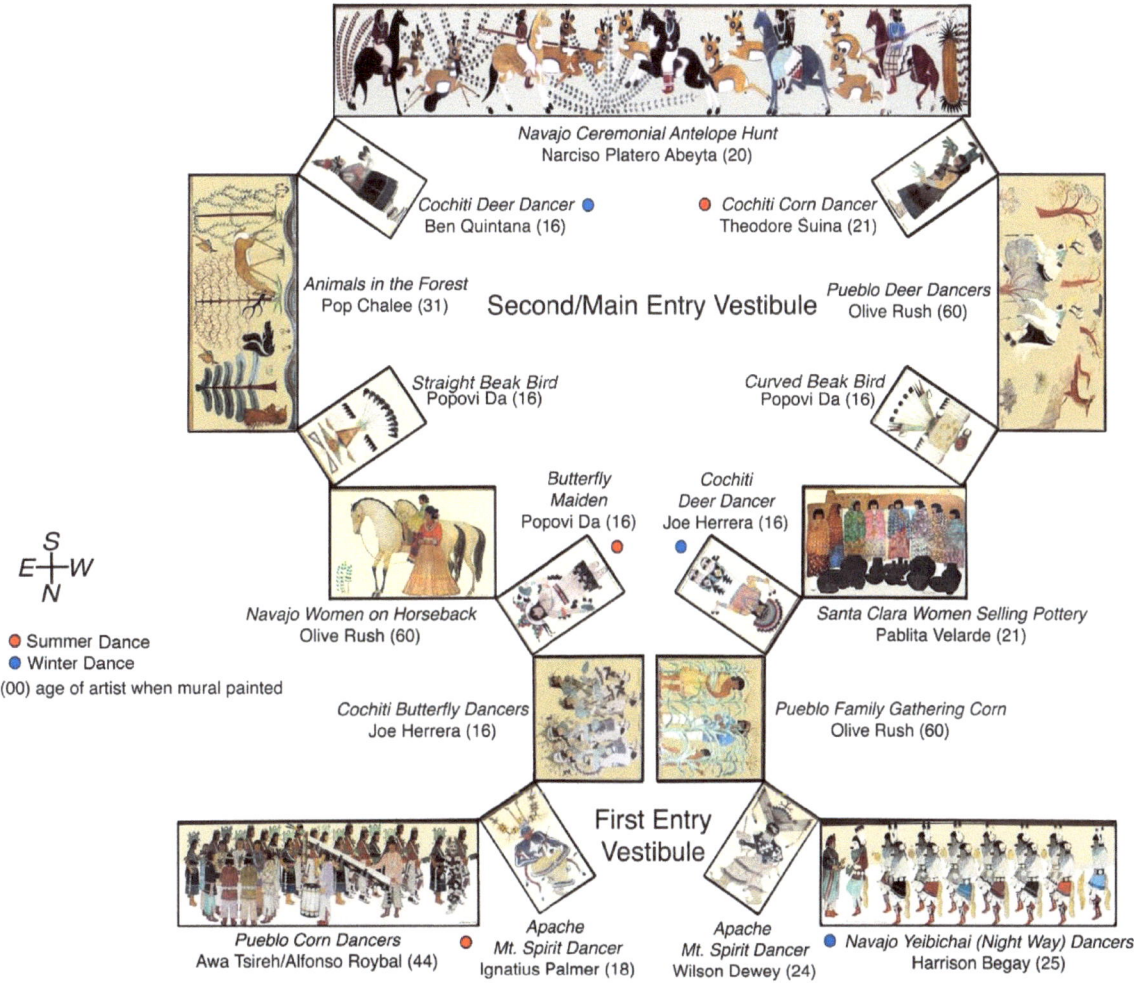

# CHAPTER EIGHT:
# THE MURALS

The remainder of this book is a presentation of the Maisel's Murals in a digitally restored form. A number of images have been grouped on facing pages as opposing pairs, in keeping with their original layout concept. Background data, as well as general descriptive information about each image contained in the 2018 publication about the Murals has been included here only in a summary manner for context. This text is focused on insights into the Mural's characteristics and context data about the subjects shown.

It is important to note that Olive Rush made certain that credit for the Maisel's Murals was given to the individual artists. Each mural is prominently signed by the artist and the theme of the mural identified.

***Pueblo Corn Dancers.***
Alfonso Roybal, Awa Tsireh (1895–1955):

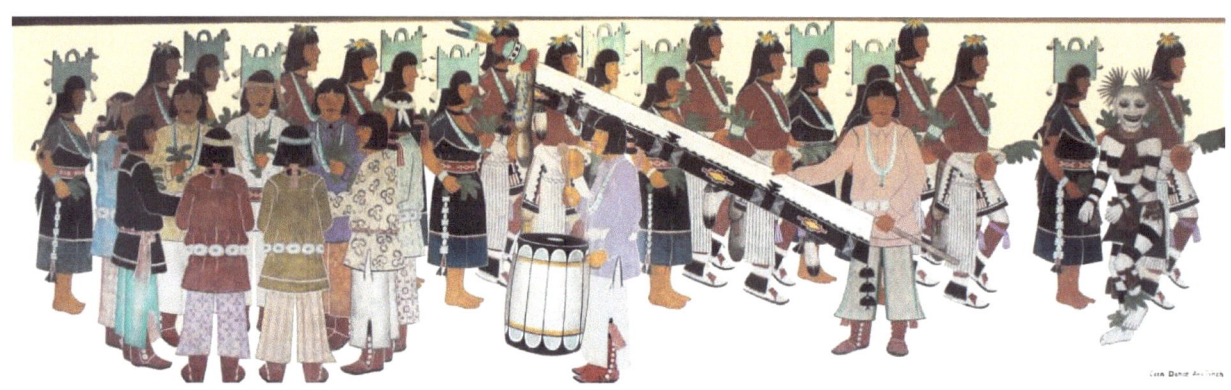

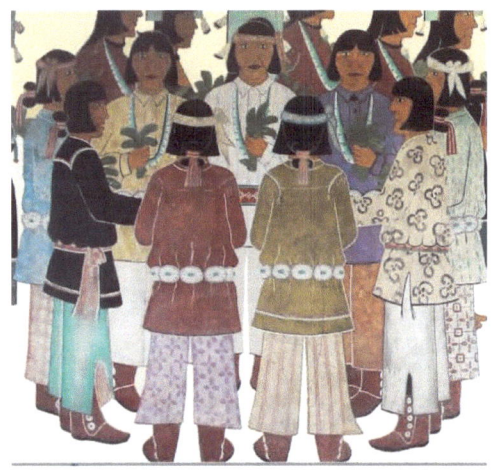

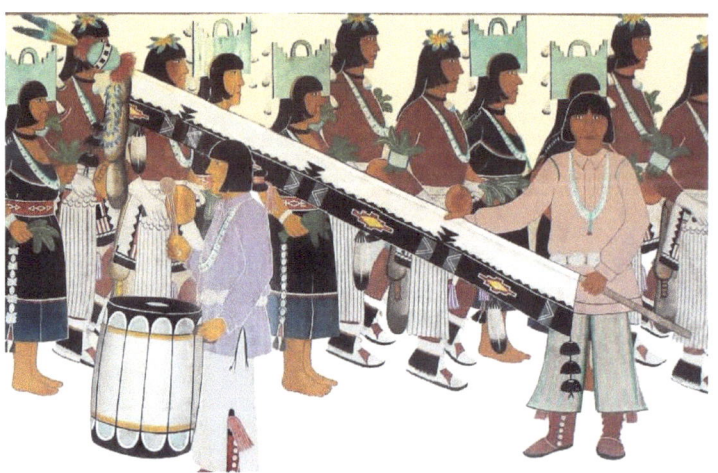

All nineteen of the Rio Grande Pueblos conduct corn dances, with the largest being on each of their Saint's Day. These are very sacred, as well as public affairs, with visitors from throughout the region, Native Americans and others come to partake in the festivities. Food is available in many houses and anyone at the dance who is invited into a house is welcome and will be fed. These dances also include numerous vendors and at the largest have an area for carnival games and rides. Usually vendors are from other Pueblos, as a significant number people from the host Pueblo, will be dancing.

At some dances there can be as many as a thousand dancers. Men and women typically dance in pairs, with children bringing up the rear. Usually there are two groups ("moieties") of dancers, identified as either turquoise or pumpkin who trade off dancing all day long. The men in this painting are brown indicating that they are of the pumpkin moiety. The turquoise moiety dancers are painted blue. Each group will have its own chorus and drum(s). The drums area each named and held in great reverence. The chorus is male. The one shown here on the left has only nine members, but at a large feast day such as the one at Kewa Pueblo, the largest of the Pueblo corn dances, there will be more than fifty singers. They will sing songs composed specially for the dance at hand, as well as songs specific to their Pueblo, and possible even a song from another Pueblo in an entirely different language.

Dance steps and formations include a single line of paired men and women moving between plazas within the Pueblo. Women carry spruce boughs in both hands, while men carry a rattle in one hand and a bough in the other. Women go barefoot and men wear moccasins typically made of deerskin suede with rawhide soles. The women's head-piece, called a tableta, is made of painted wood, to which eagle down is attached, or perhaps turkey feathers, as shown in this case. The men are wearing white dance kilts with a nearly uniform embroidered design, only glimpses of which are visible in this painting. They have skunk skin anklets, parrot feathers on top of their heads, and, while not visible here fox or coyote skins hanging from the back of their belts. In subsection **8. Engaging the Viewer** there is a discussion of the black and white stripped kossa (ceremonial clown.)

The banner held by a special carrier is made of a long embroidered sash, with macaw feathers atop a carved and painted ball. Whatever the complex, secret symbolism, we can be certain that the dance is about fertility, growth, auspicious weather, and most importantly bringing and maintaining balance at the Pueblo and throughout the world.

**Blueface Navajo Yébîchai Nightway Dancers.**
Harrison Begay; Haashke yah Niya (The Wandering Boy); (1914–2012):

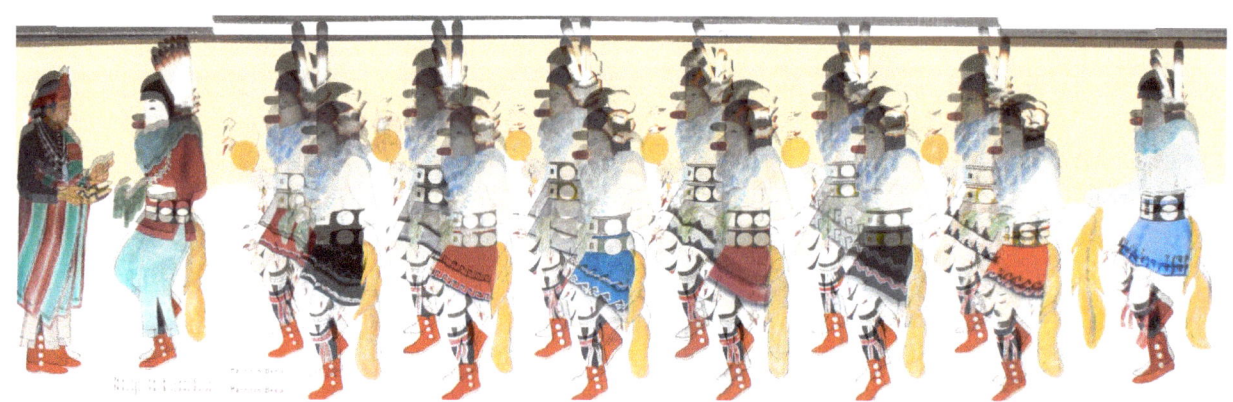
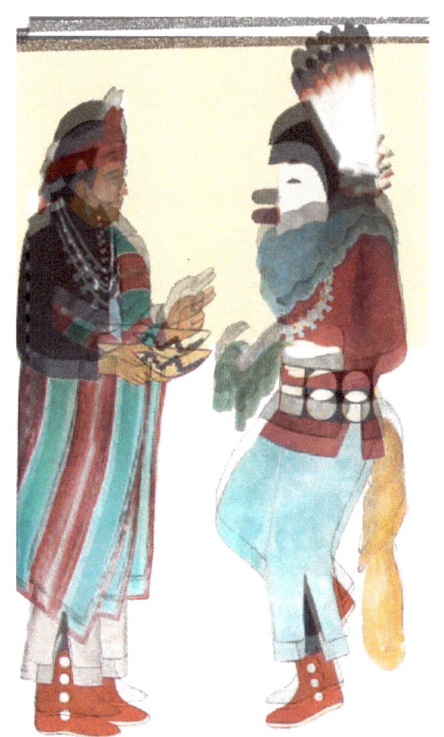
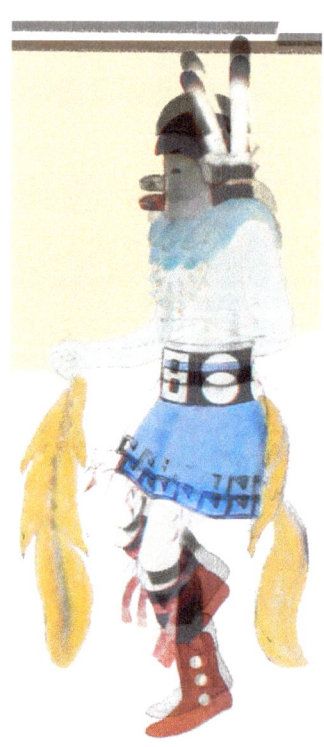

In this painting we see the conclusion of the Nightway ceremony, the most important of a number of nine-day winter healing ceremonies. Nearly all the important characters of the Diné (Navajo) pantheon are mentioned in legends, depicted in sand paintings, and impersonated with the use of masks and other ritual objects. The dancers are personifications of the supernatural beings called *yei*. The masked white face dancer at the front impersonates *Yebichai*, maternal grandfather of the *yei* and one of the manifestations of *Haashch'eeti'i*, Talking God.

The ceremonial leader is called a *hataałii* (singer) who is a trained specialist in usually no more than one or two of the more than two dozen ceremonies called "ways." This is because each way is a vast complex of hundreds of songs, prayers, medicines, sand paintings, and various ritual acts which must be preformed flawlessly. A number of these ways have died out when the last singer who knew the ceremony died.

There are six pairs of dancers, typically male and female. The figure at the rear is *Tó'neníli*, Water Sprinkler, a mischievous rain god. However, the figures as seen here may not be portrayed as they would appear in an actual dance.

Navajo and Pueblo ceremonies are quite different, although the ultimate purpose of maintaining wellbeing and balance is essentially the same. It is the emphasis of the ceremony that is different. Unlike the Pueblos, the Diné practice is more individualistic with ceremonies primarily conducted for individual curing and preventing disease. Pueblo ceremonies are thoroughly integrated with the community's social organization and are primarily to bring good weather and for fertility, with curing of secondary importance. In addition, unlike the Diné, Pueblo ceremonies are carried out in an annual cycle according to a calendar and carried out by organized priesthoods, religious societies, or other groups. The focus for the Pueblos is on the common good of the community as a whole, and the individual is subordinated.

The differences seem to clearly relate to one culture, Pueblo, being sedentary and agricultural and the other, whose ancestors in prehistoric times were hunter/gatherer nomads. While Diné ceremonies include considerable esoteric and secret, hence dangerous, knowledge, the Diné are much more open than the Pueblos to sharing specific information about a given ceremony to a trusted individual. A key difference is that Diné ceremonies are private and you must be invited to attend, rather than large public gatherings such as a Pueblo Feast Day.

*Apache Mountain Spirit Dancer.*
l. Ignatius Palmer (1922–1985) and r. Wilson Dewey (1915–1969):

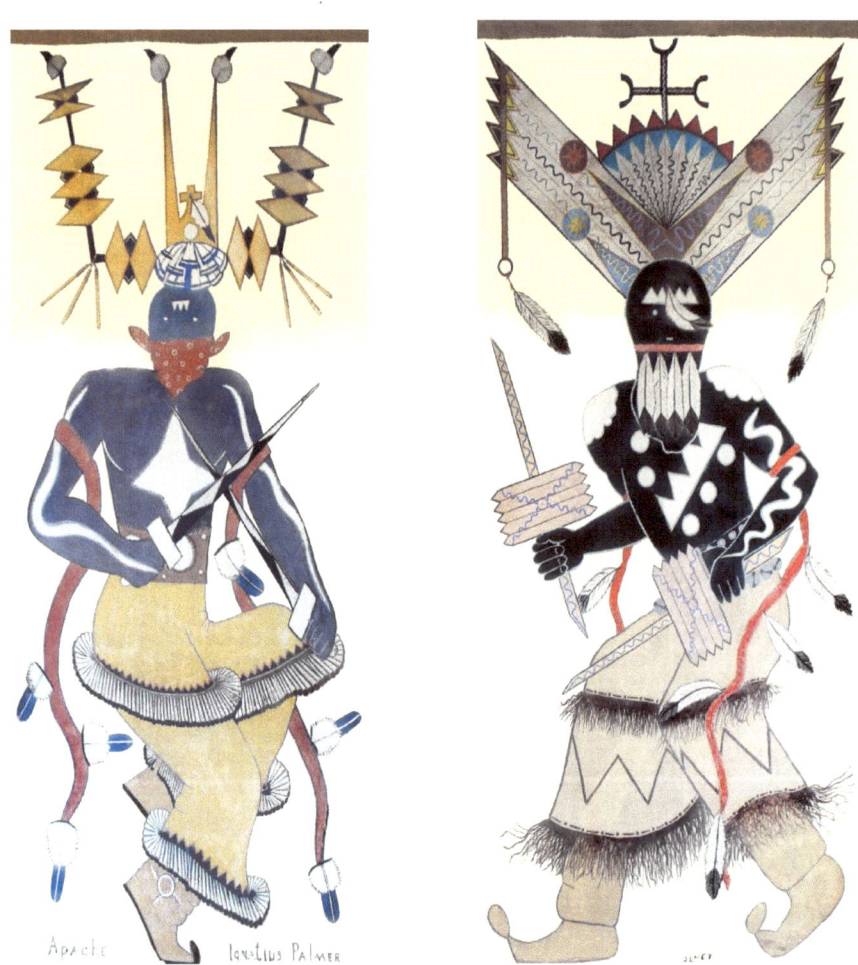

These individual figures represent one of a grouping of dancers that appear at night around a massive bonfire as part a girls puberty ritual. Palmer's figure indicates the high step of the dancer, while Dewey's figure has turned to more directly confront the viewer. Both Palmer and Dewey are Chiricahua Apache with Palmer being from the Mescalero Reservation in New Mexico and Dewey is from the San Carlos Reservation in Arizona.

### *Straight Beaked Bird* and *Curved Billed Bird*
Tony Martinez, Popovi Da (Red Fox), (1922–1971):

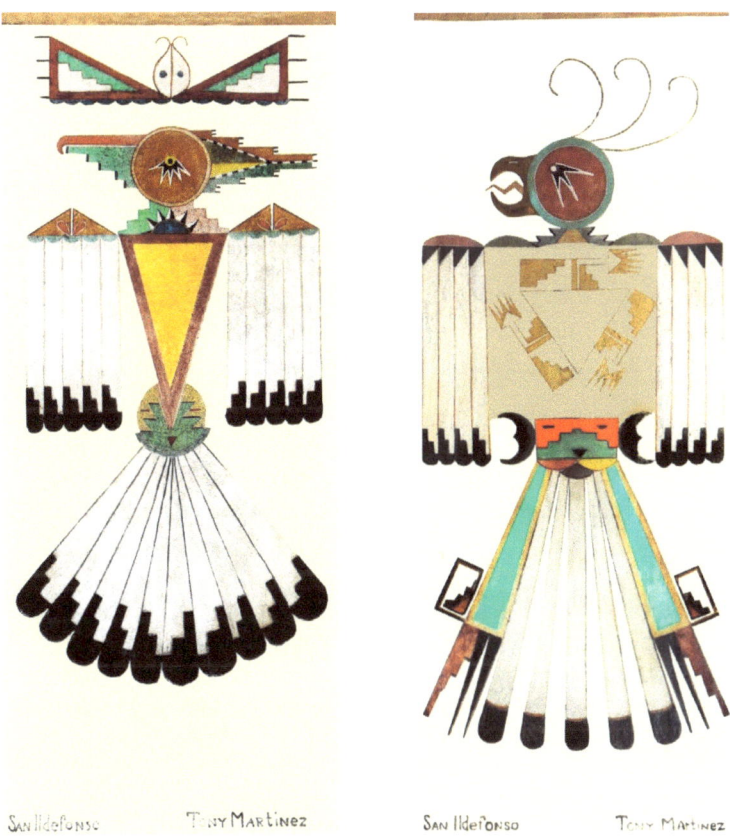

These birds are often interpreted as Thunderbirds, but Thunderbirds are Northwest Coast symbolism and not Southwestern. They might more appropriately be called Rain Birds. However, they are probably more influenced by "Indian" images that tourists found appealing. While birds are a common motif in Pueblo art, such birds are typically highly stylized forms found on pottery (like the designs found on the chest of the curved billed bird), from the prehistoric to modern times, or based on actual birds such as the straight billed birds typical of Zia Pueblo and the curved bill parrots found on Acoma pottery. These birds are clearly mythological, with their white and black eagle feathers that come from young Golden Eagles (*Aquila chrysaetos*), faces at the base of their tails and various other symbolic Pueblo design motifs. Wherever they may have originally come from they are certainly Southwestern Pueblo now.

*Cochiti Butterfly Dancers.*
**Joe H. Herrera; See Ru (Blue Bird); (1923–2001):**

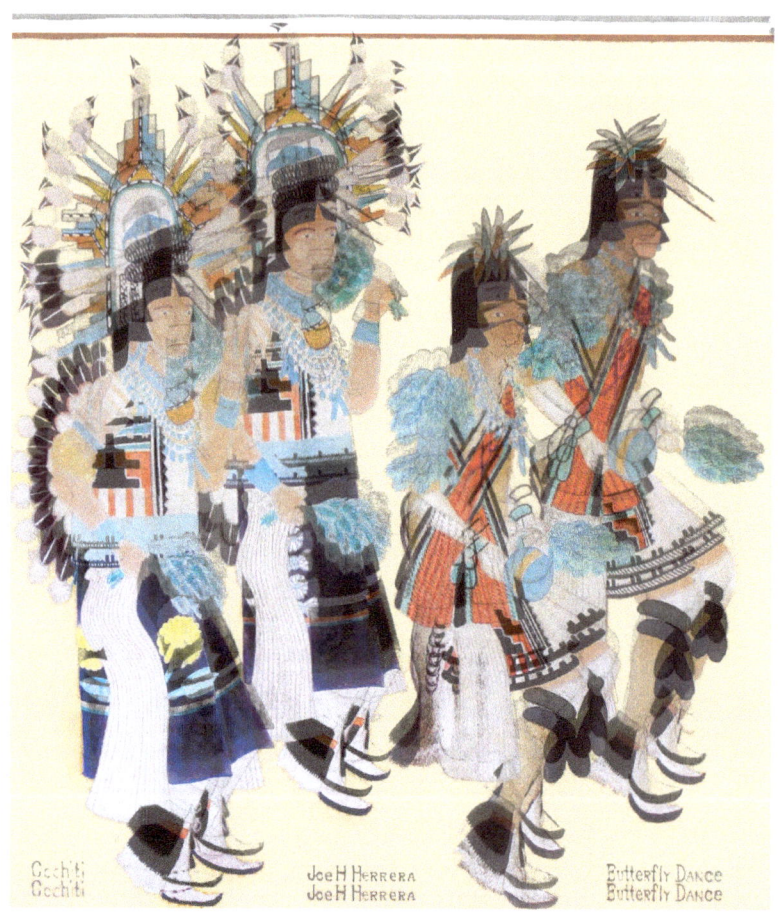

The butterfly dance is a Pueblo social dance, i.e. open to the whole community and visitors, held in August or September near the end of the harvest. It is a thanksgiving celebration ceremony for the harvest, especially for the corn crop. The dance is performed at the New Mexico Pueblos and is also popular at the Hopi villages in Arizona. Herrera's painting is in the strict *The Studio* style. It shows two pairs of male and female dancers of what would be a large grouping. Their dance regalia is shown in great detail; see the discussion of *Pueblo Corn Dancers* by Awa Tsireh for an explanation of what they are wearing.

## Pueblo Family Gathering Corn.
Olive Rush (1873-1966)

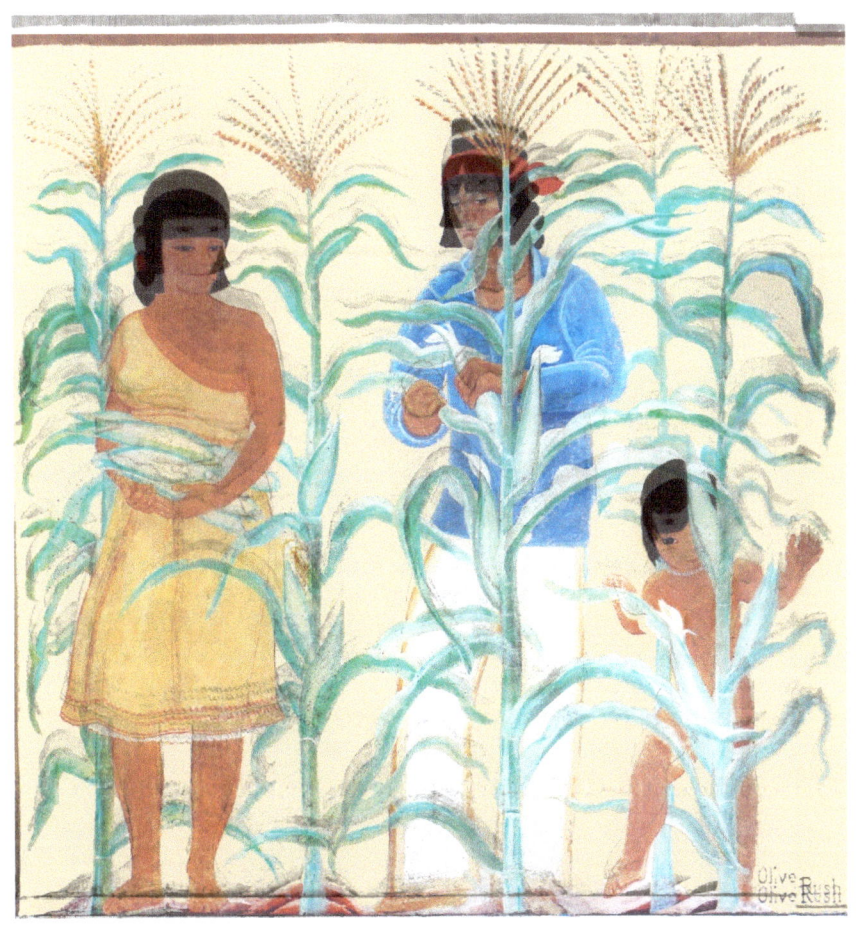

This is the first of three of the Maisel Murals painted by Olive Rush. It is a nuclear family scene that will fit well with the Anglo viewers understanding of an ideal family and "Indianness" as depicted by corn. Rush's painting at first glance appears be in *The Studio* style, but this is only an facade. As mentioned previously, her paintings were strongly influenced by European, Persian and Asian graphic styles and techniques in their composition and execution, as well as with color variations and suggestions of perspective. This family scene, and the following *Navajo Women on Horseback*, allude to very Western notions of family that contrast significantly with the family seen in Pablita Velarde's *Santa Clara Women Selling Pottery*.

*Navajo Women on Horseback*
Olive Rush (1873-1966)

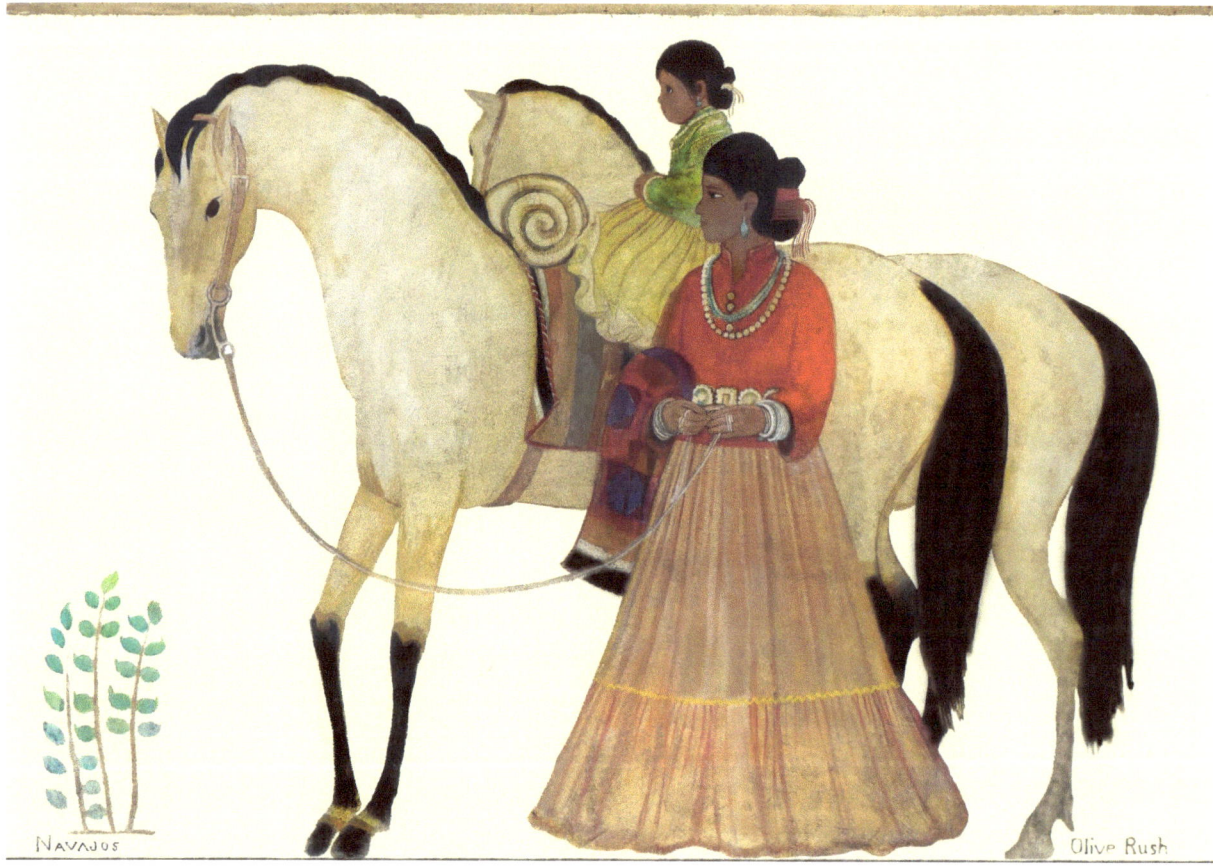

As with Rush's Pueblo Deer Dancers mural on page 37, this painting shows strong Asian influences. The horses look like Chinese Tang Dynasty ceramics. The scene of mother and child is a romantic view of the Navajo, instantly recognizable and emotionally appealing. It comes close to being kitsch, if not for the quality and uniqueness of the painting style. This mural pairs with Pablita Velarde's highly personal *Santa Clara Women Selling Pottery*. Note the similar color palettes of these two paintings.

*Santa Clara Women Selling Pottery.*
Pablita Velarde, Tse Twan (Golden Dawn), (1918–2006):

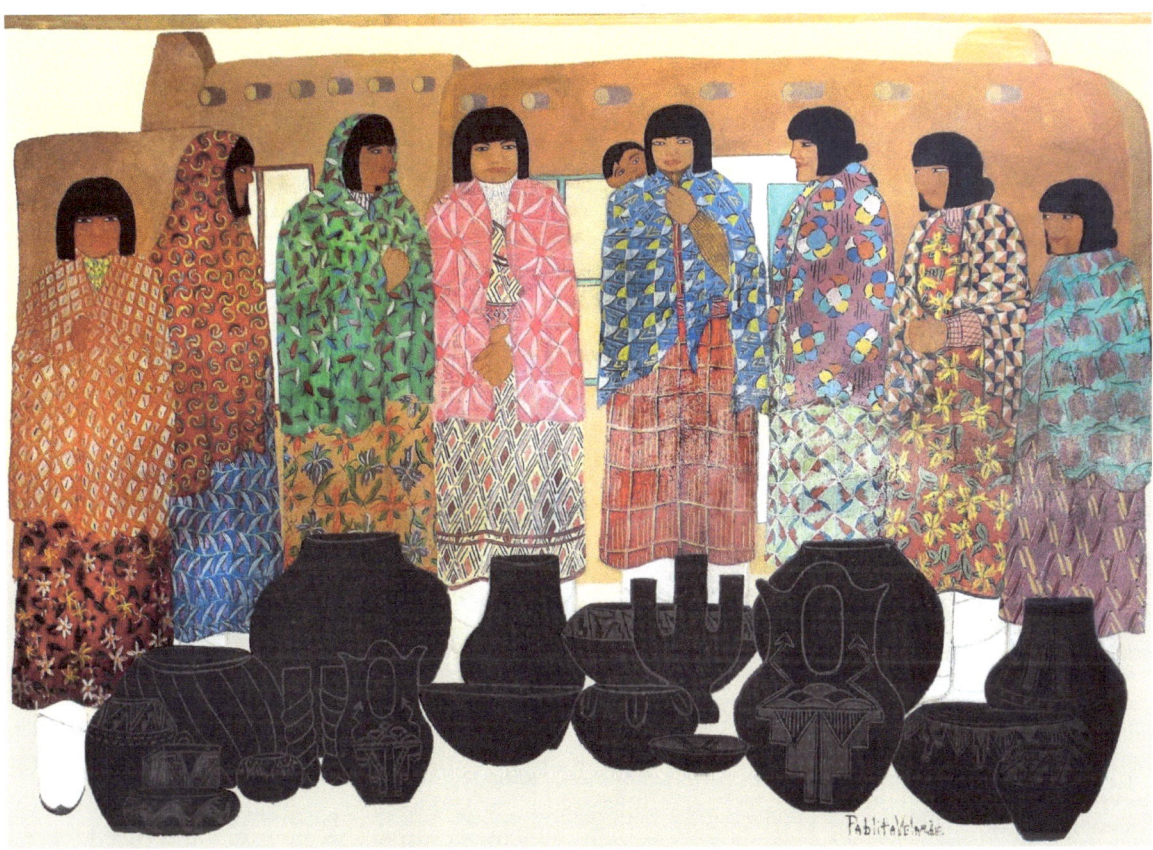

As we have already seen in subsections **5. Precision and Detail** and **8. Engaging the Viewer** there is a lot going on with this image. At first glance it is primarily decorative with colorful cotton print garments contrasted by the black forms of the pottery in front and the pueblo house (the only mural depicting a dwelling) behind the figures. I think this is a family group with a self-portrait of Velarde and her three sisters who were potters, also in the painting. Sisters Lucaria (Jane) Baca and Legoria Tafoya are in pink and blue in the middle and third sister Rosita Tsosie at the far right. Their grandmother and teacher, Margaret Tafoya, a seminal figure in Santa Clara pottery, may be the figure in profile in a mostly purple garment. This is solely my personal conjecture. Interestingly, none of the carved pottery or animal figures associated with Santa Clara pottery are shown. This painting was painted over three days in mid-April 1939, see Appendix C for a look at Santa Clara Pueblo in 1940.

## Animals in a Forest.
### Merina Lujan Hopkins; Pop Chalee (Blue Flower); (1906–1993):

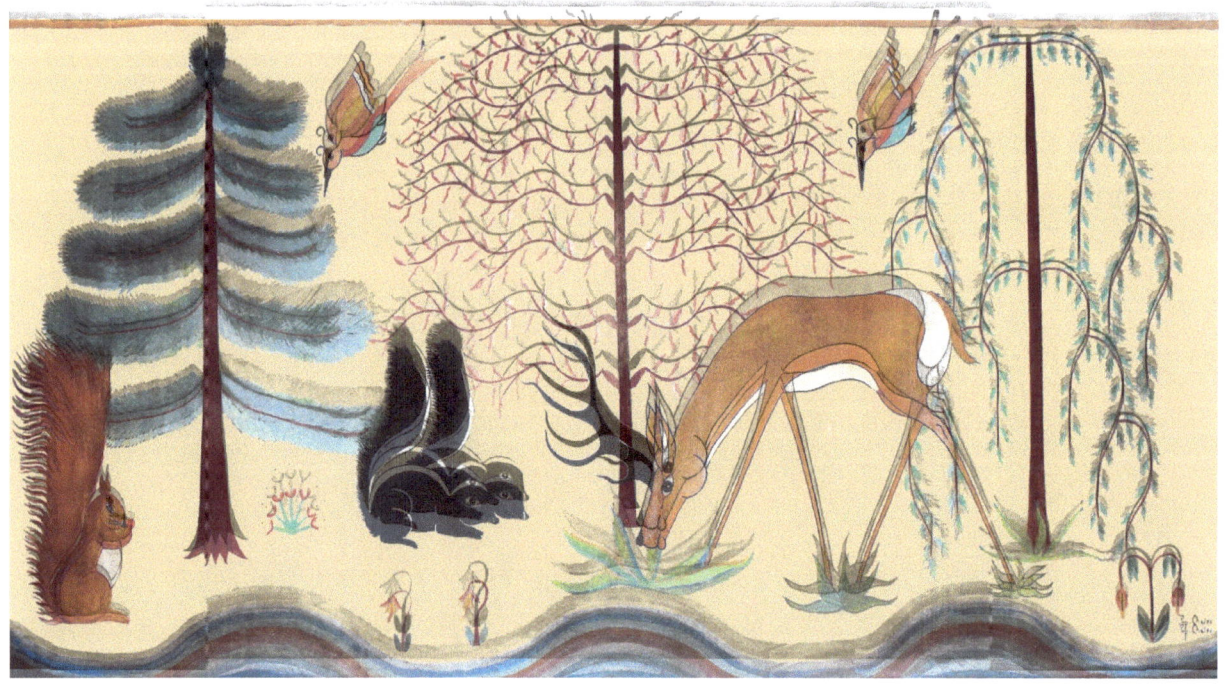

Wherever this forest is, it is not New Mexico. The pine tree on the left and the willow on the right fit with New Mexico, but the tree in the middle is something of an enigma. Striped skunks are found throughout North America. I wanted the squirrel to be a tufted eared New Mexico Abert's Squirrel (Sciurus aberti); but the New Mexico subspecies are black or gray with prominent ear tufts. This squirrel looks much more like a European Red Squirrel (Sciurus vulgaris). The birds are imaginary with a combination of features not found on any living bird. The deer is very Bambi like, following puberty. Its patterning does not follow that of a living deer. North American Mule Deer have white rumps but also white tails with a black tip. And in the end, does any of this somewhat tortured assessment really matter all that much. I include it here only to contrast the unique iconoclast world Pop Chalee created with the hyper realistic Pueblo world of Awa Tsireh and his generation. It should be noted that the Disney "Bambi" film came out in 1942. Pop Chalee's magical forest scenes were included at an exhibition at Stanford University in California in 1936 and Disney visited this show. He also visited the Santa Fe Indian School in 1936 and purchased one of the Chalee's forest scenes. When Disney offered her a job, she declined saying that she didn't want to spend her art career painting Mickey Mouse hands. For all their "cuteness," Chalee created a mystical world with a uniquely Native American sensibility.

# Pueblo Deer Dancers
## Olive Rush (1873-1966)

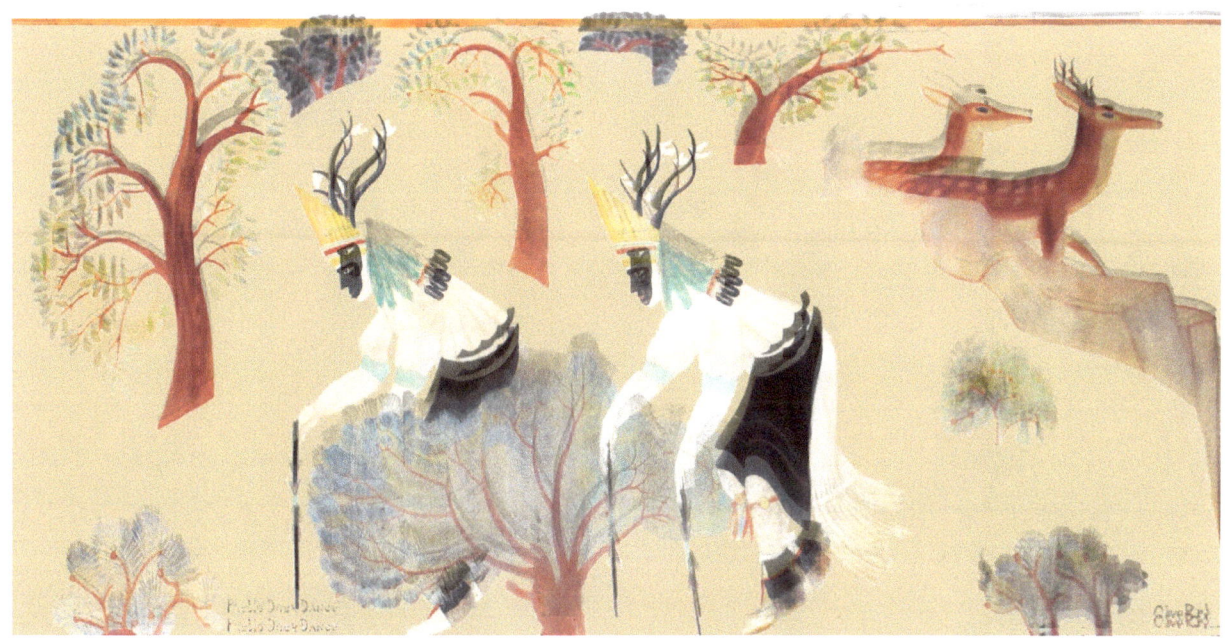

At the opposite end of Maisel's inner foyer from Pop Chalee's forest scene is this forest scene of *Pueblo Deer Dancers*. The dancers are Tewa inspired deer dancers, part of the Winter Dance cycle of animal dances. They come into the Pueblo early in the morning from the surrounding mountains and dance throughout the day. At the conclusion of the dance they are sometimes ritually shot and carried out of the Plaza, after their last breath has been taken in by the hunter. But then there is the forest. Like Chalee's forest, this one does not exist in New Mexico. But rather than a mythical Chalee forest this one appears to be a real forest. There are strong east Asian influences in the painting, from the depiction of the trees and rocks, to the deer.

***Butterfly Maiden* (l) and *Cochiti Woman Dear Dancer* (r)**
Tony Martinez, Popovi Da (Red Fox), (1922–1971) and Joe H. Herrera, See Ru (Blue Bird), (1923–2001*)*:

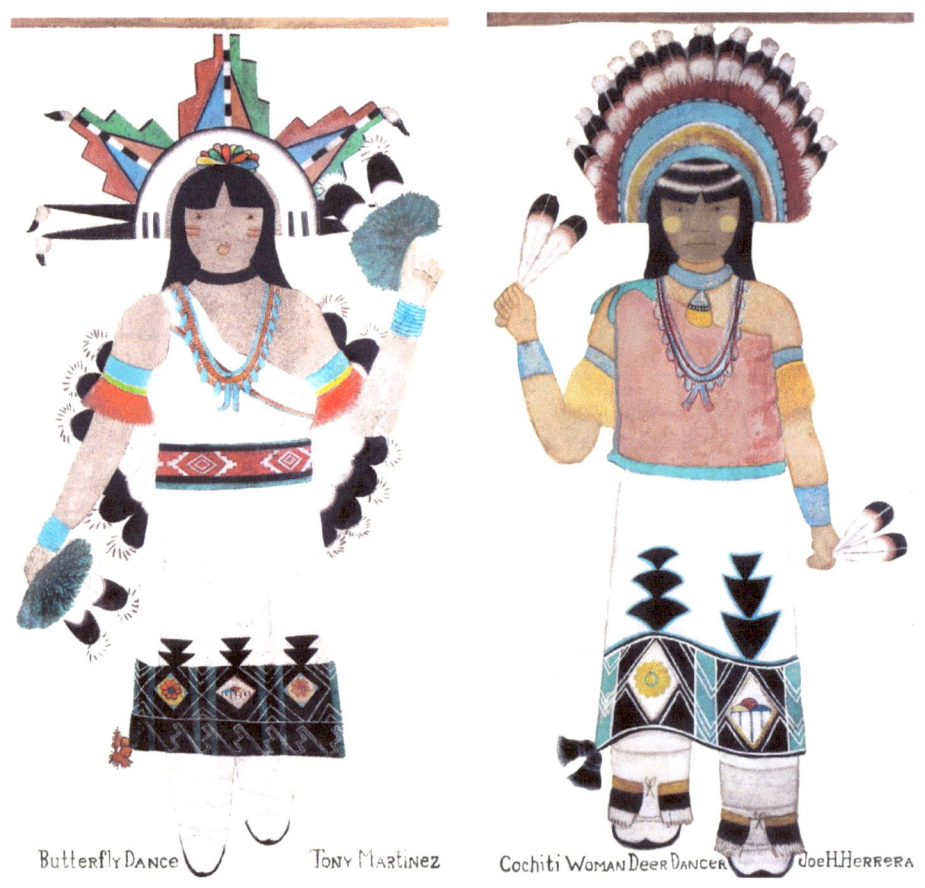

The frontal view of these female dancers follow the strict guidelines of *The Studio* style, although both artists were only sixteen when they painted these figures. As with the two female dance figures on the following page, these dancers at first appear very similar, but when taking a closer look are quite different. Compare Herrera's dancer here with Quintana's dancer from the same dance on the following page. They are wearing essentially the same regalia, although one wears an embroidered manta and one a plain black Pueblo style skirt.

***Cochiti Deer Dancer* (l) and *Cochiti Corn Dancer* (r)**
Ben Quintana, Há-ā- tee, (1923–1944) and Theodore Suina, Ku-Pe-Ru (Snow), (1918–aft. 2018?):

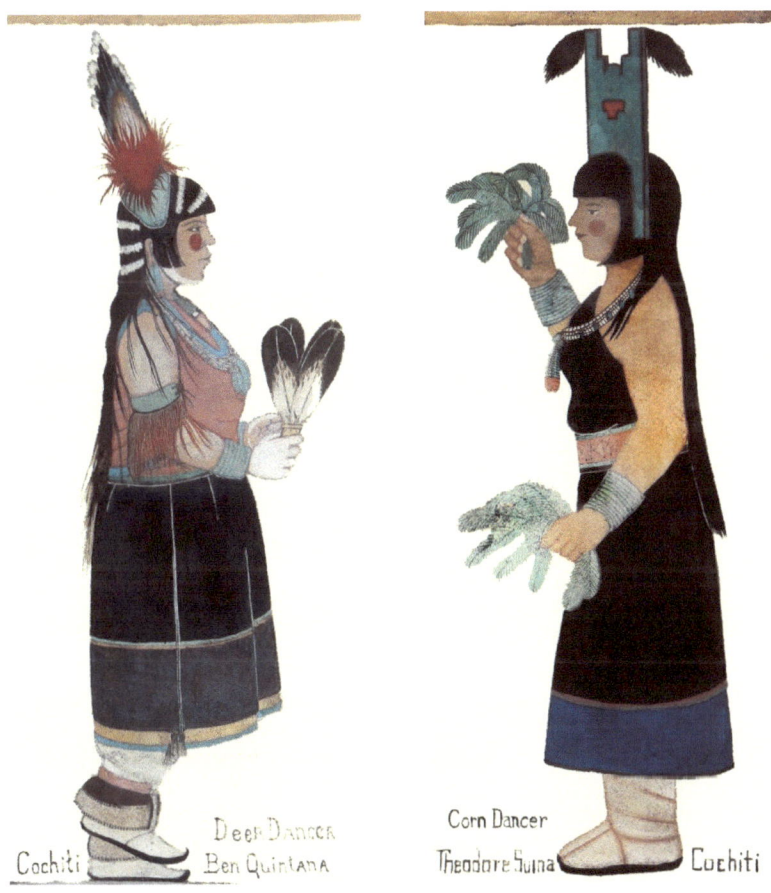

These opposing female Cochiti dancers are similar, but once again like the previous dancers are on further study quite different. The Deer Dancer has a painted tableta with eagle feathers, white stripes in her hair, carries eagle feathers and has skunk ruff anklets over the wrappings of her deerskin moccasins. The Corn Dancer has a simpler tableta, with no painting on her hair, carries spruce boughs, and lacks the skunk ankle ruffs. Note the precision, detail and expression of sixteen year old Quintana's work, contrasted with the much less expressive flat surface of twenty-one year old Suina's work.

*Navajo Ceremonial Antelope Hunt*.
**Narciso Platero Abeyta; Ha-So-De; (1918–1998):**

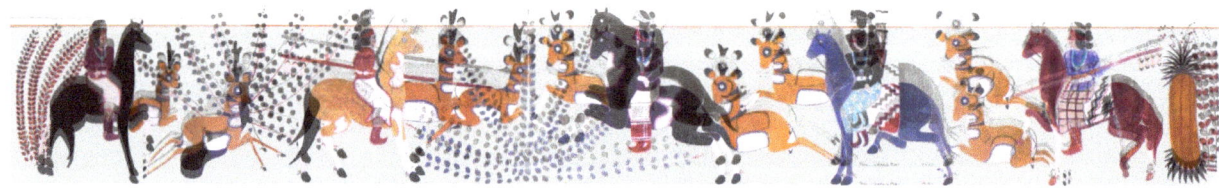

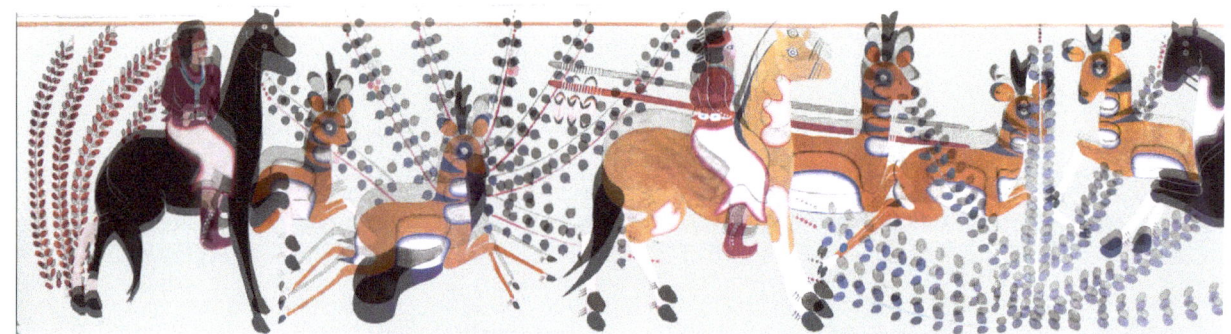

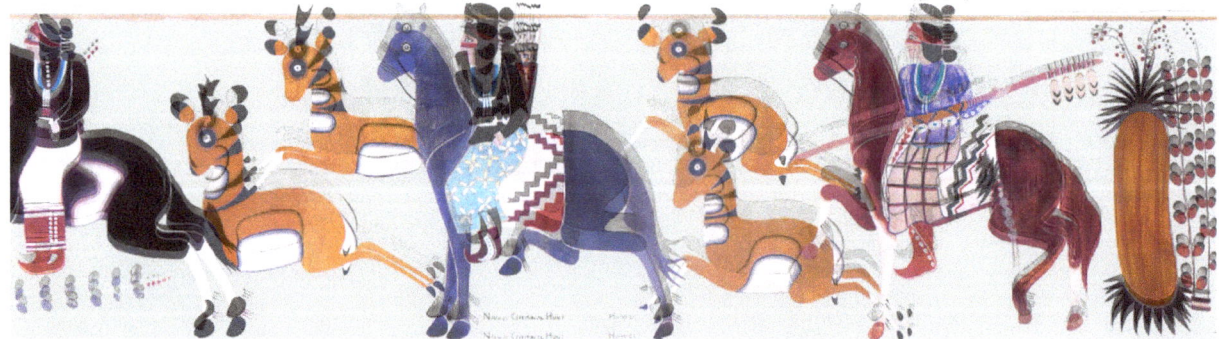

Ha-So-De painted this theme on a number of occasions. The painting exhibits his restrained color palette of blacks, browns, and ochre with a few red accents. Art historian Clara Lee Tanner notes that he was more interested in "bold effects than in minute detail." This is clearly the most modern/progressive of the Maisel's Murals and while representative of *The Studio* style diverges from that style in terms of viewer orientation, in that the viewer seems to be on the ground with vegetation in the foreground looking up at the scene. The Diné will understand themes of life and death associated with hunting in this image that will not be understood by Anglo viewers.

# REFERENCES

Bernstein, Bruce and Rushing III, W. Jackson.
1995 *Modern by Tradition: American Indian Painting in The Studio Style*. Santa Fe, New Mexico: Museum of New Mexico Press.

Brody, J. J.
1971 *Indian Painters and White Patrons*. Albuquerque, New Mexico: University of New Mexico Press.
1997 *Pueblo Indian Painting/Tradition and Modernism in New Mexico. 1900–1930*, Santa Fe, New Mexico: School of American Research Press.

Cesa, Margaret,
2008 *The World of Flower Blue: Pop Chalee: An Artistic Biography*. Santa Fe, New Mexico: Red Crane Books, Art Series.

Chase, Katherine L.,
2001 *Indian Painters of the Southwest: The Deep Remembering*. Santa Fe, New Mexico: School of American Research Press.

Dawdy, Doris Ostrander,
1968 *Annotated Bibliography of American Indian Painting*. Museum of the American Indian, Heye Foundation, Vol. XXI, Part 2, New York, New York.

Dunn, Dorothy,
1951 *The Development of Modern American Painting in the Southwest and Plains Area*. El Palacio Magazine, Vol. 58, No. 11: Santa Fe, New Mexico.
1962 *Contemporary Indian Painting from the Margretta S. Dietrich Collection*. Catalog/essay for an exhibit by the American Embassy: Washington DC, 1962.
1968 *American Indian Painting of the Southwest and Plains Areas*. University of New Mexico Press: Albuquerque, New Mexico.

Duwe, Samuel Gregg
2011 *The Prehispanic Tewa World, Space, Time and Becoming in the Pueblo Southwest*, A Dissertation Submitted to the School of Anthropology, University of Arizona.

Gilmore, Jann Haynes
2016 *Olive Rush Finding Her Place in the Santa Fe Art Colony,* Museum of New Mexico Press, Santa Fe, New Mexico.

Hahn, Milanne Shelburne,
2011 *The Studio Painting at the Santa Fe Indian School: A Case Study in Modern American Identity,* Dissertation for Doctor of Philosophy, The University of Texas: Austin, Texas.

Horton, Jessica L.
2015 "A Cloudburst in Venice: Fred Kabotie and the U. S. Pavilion of 1932," *American Art* Vol. 29, no. 1, pp. 54-81, The University of Chicago.

Horton, Jessica L. and Berlo, Janet Catherine
2015 "Pueblo Painting in 1932 - Folding Narratives of Native Art in American Art History", published in *A Companion to American Art,* pp. 266 - 280, John Wiley & Sons, Inc.

Jacobson, Oscar Brousse and d'Ucel, Jeanne.
1950 *American Indian Painters, Volume II.* Editions D'Art, C. Szwedzicki Publisher: Nice, France.

Kammer, David J.,
1993 National Register of Historic Places, Multiple Property Documentation Form, *Historic and Architectural Resources of Route 66 Through New Mexico*: Washington, DC, October 1993.

Matthews, Washington,
1902 (2002 edition) *The Night Chant: A Navajo Ceremony,* University of Utah Press, Salt Lake City, Utah.

National Register of Historic Places, *Maisel's Indian Trading Post.* #93001215,
1993 Washington DC.

Lester, Patrick D, *The Biographical Directory of Native American Painters.*
1995 SIR Publications: Tulsa, Oklahoma.

Rush, Olive,
2004    *Olive Rush Papers, 1879–1967: Series 4: Records of Artwork, 1933–1956,* Box 3, Folder 8; and *Series 7: Photographs circa 1890–1966: Rush and Native American Artists Painting Frescoes at Maisel's Indian Trading Post, Albuquerque, NM, 1939,* Box 6, Folder 14; Smithsonian Institute, Archives of American Art: Washington DC.

Secord, Paul R.;
2012    *Albuquerque Deco and Pueblo.* Arcadia Publishing: Charleston, South Carolina, 2012.
2018    *The Maisel's Murals 1939 - Native American Art of the American Southwest.* Sunstone Press: Santa Fe, New Mexico.

Scott, Sascha T.;
2014    "Awa Tsireh and the Art of Subtle Resistance", Art Bulletin 95(4), pp. 74-80.
2020    *Ana-Ethnographic Representations: Early Modern Pueblo Painters, Scientific Colonialism, and Tactics of Refusal,* Arts.

Scott, Sascha T. and Lonetree, Amy
2020    *The Past and the Future are Now,* Arts.

Snodgrass, Jeanne O.;
1968    *American Indian Painters: A Biographical Directory.* Museum of the American Indian: New York, New York.

Spivey, Richard L.;
2003    *The Legacy of Maria Povka Martinez,* Museum of New Mexico Press: Santa Fe New Mexico.

Sweet, Jill D.
1985    *Dances of the Tewa Pueblo Indians - Expressions of New Life,* School of American Research Press, Santa Fe, New Mexico.

# Appendix A
# Maisel's Murals Artist Overview

Table 1: Maisel's Murals Artist Overview

| Artist | Sex | Cultural Affiliation | The Studio student SFIS* | WWII service | Age in April 1939 | Primary Media | April Days Painting Maisel Murals | Total Payment for Maisel Murals** |
|---|---|---|---|---|---|---|---|---|
| Narciso Abeyta (1918 – 1998) | M | Diné (Navajo) Eastern Reservation, Tohajilee, NM | yes | U.S. Army codetalker | 20 | Casein, Tempera | 11, 14, 15, 20, 22 | $30.00 (bonus) |
| Harrison Begay (1914? – 2012) | M | Diné (Navajo) Western Reservation, White Cone, AZ | yes | U.S. Army | 25 | Tempera, Oil, Watercolor, other | 11, 14, 20, 22 | $25.00 (bonus) |
| Pop Chalee / Merina Lujan Hopkins (1908 – 1993) | F | Tiwa Pueblo and Switzerland/India Taos, NM | no | no | 31 | Tempera, Oil, Watercolor | not recorded | $32.50 paintings; $12.50 hotel bill |
| Wilson Dewey (1915 – 1969) | M | Chiricahua Apache San Carlos Res., AZ | yes | U.S. Army | 24 | Gouache, Tempera | 11 | $5.00 (bonus) |
| Joe H. Herrera (1923 – 2001) | M | Keresan Pueblo Cochiti, NM | yes | U.S. Army | 16 | Tempera, Oil, Watercolor | 11, 14, 15, 22 | $18.50 (bonus) |
| Tony Martinez (1923 – 1971) | M | Tewa Pueblo San Ildefonso, NM | yes | U.S. Army | 16 | Pottery, watercolor | 11, 14, 22, 25 | $15.00 (bonus) |
| Ignatius Palmer (1922 – 1985) | M | Chiricahua Apache Mescalero Res., NM | yes | U.S. Army Air Corps | 18 | Casein, Tempera | 20, 22 | $7.00 (bonus) |
| Ben Quintana (1921-1944) | M | Keresan Pueblo Cochiti, NM | yes | posthumous silver star | 16 | Gouache | 22 | $5.00 (bonus) |
| Awa Tsireh / Alfonso Roybal (1898 – 1955) | M | Tewa Pueblo San Ildefonso, NM | no | no | 44 | Gouache, Tempera, Watercolor, other | 10, 11, 14, 22, 29 | $91.00 |
| Theodore Suina (1918 – ) | M | Keresan Pueblo Cochiti, NM | yes | U.S. Navy | 21 | Gouache | 22 | $5.00 (bonus) |
| Pablita Velarde (1918 – 2006) | F | Tewa Pueblo Santa Clara, NM | no | no | 21 | Casein, gouache, tempera or watercolor | not recorded | $40.00 |
| Olive Rush (1873 – 1966) | F | Anglo | no | no | 66 | Fresco, Oil, Gouache, Mixed-Media, Stained Glass, Watercolor | 10, 11, 14, 15, 20, 22, 29 | About $500 for three paintings of $1,500 total contract |

* This column indicates artists who were students of the SFIS *The Studio* arts program at the time the Maisel Murals were painted, both Pop Chalee and Pablita Velarde had previously been *The Studio* students, and Awa Tsireh had assisted with some *The Studio* programs.

** The SFIS Arts and Crafts Fund was paid $330 for the student work on the Maisel Murals, with either $8 or $10 allotted to Geronima Cruz Montoya, the director of the SFIS arts program for her assistance with the mural project. "Bonuses" were paid by Olive Rush from her total contract amount, as none of the monies paid to the SFIS went to the student artists.

Prepared by Paul R. Secord based on genealogical research using US census, death records, obituaries, military records and related sources from Ancestry.com, Find a Grave, and various tribal records. Thanks to Wynona Tashio, granddaughter of Ignatius Palmer who verified he was a Chiricahua Apache. Payment information, Maisel painting dates and identification of SFIS mural artists from the Olive Rush Archives, Smithsonian Institute.

**Appendix B**
**Technical Information on the Images Used in this Book**

All of the images used in this book were taken by the author, Paul R. Secord, in September 2015 or November 2017, using a Canon EOS T3 camera with an EFS 18-55 mm lens as RAW 4272 X 2848 resolution images that were processed as Tiff files. Some parallax correction was made using Photoshop soon after the images were initially taken, and again checked during the processing of the images for this book. The digital restoration was accomplished using Photoshop CS6, version 13.0 x64 on a Macintosh 27-in desktop computer.

## Appendix C
## Santa Clara Pueblo in 1940 and the Velarde Family

**1940 US Census - Santa Clara Potters** (Those who were identified as a pottery maker on this Census) Election Precinct 26 Ranchitos, Santa Clara Pueblo (Part), 28 Espanola, Santa Clara Pueblo (part). Pablita Velarde Census Enumerator April 8 - 11, 1940.

That Pablita Velarde was the census enumerator is of key importance. She identified many of the females by their matrilineal name, shown in parenthesis, as well as by their husbands surname line. This is in keeping with Pueblo linage conventions that would probably not have been recognized by an Anglo census taker. She also noted the "professions" of women. Pottery making was a skill that was expected of women, although there are three males listed as potters in the 1940 census. This was an essential skill in the well into the historic period, but by 1940 was more associated with supplemental income from tourists, rather that utilitarian household use. Pablita identified herself in a single person household as an artist with her own studio at the Pueblo.

In 1940:
416 person total Native American population at Santa Clara Pueblo.
82 total households
50 persons identified as a pottery maker of which 20 are Tafoya or Tafoya/Naranjo and 13 are Naranjo or Naranjo/Tafoya.

Chavarria, Fransia 32
Guiterrez (Montoya) Petra 34
Guiterrez, Faustia 41
Guiterrez, Lola 44
Guiterrez, Lupita 27
**Naranjo** (Guiterrez), Madelina 23
**Naranjo** (Herrera). Domingita 52
**Naranjo** (Padilla), Benarita 17
**Naranjo**, Cristina 44
**Naranjo**, Eva 23
**Naranjo**, Margaret 21
**Naranjo**, Mariana 42
**Naranjo**, Molly 26

Naranjo, Nicolasia 32
Naranjo, Sarita 30
Naranjo, Terescita 20
Naranjo (Tafoya) Flora 26
Naranjo (Tafoya); Barbarita 24
Padilla, Rayeita 31
Silva, Nastora 50
Sipla, Helen 21
Sisneros, Apolonia 45
Sisneros, Clara 33
Sisneros, Elena 60
Sisneros, Olaria 31
Sisneros, Victoriano 67 (male)
Swazo, Candelaria 50
Swazo, Clarita 25
Swazon, Maria 24
Chauarria, (Tafoya), Pablita 36
Guiterrez (Tafoya); Dorita 25
Guiterrez (Tafoya), Rebecca 70
Padilla (Tafoya); Dolanita 40
Tapia (Tafoya) Belen 23
Tafoya (Naranjo) Lorencito 40
Tafoya (Naranjo) Lucaria 46
Tafoya (Naranjo); Clarita 47
Tafoya (Naranjo); Patricina 40
Tafoya, Agapita 26
Tafoya, Camillo 36 (male)
Tafoya, Legaria 29
Tafoya, Madglina 27
Tafoya, Margaret 36
Tafoya, Maria 40
Tafoya, Mary 38h
Tafoya, Petra 41
Tafoya, Placida 60
Tafoya, Severa 49
Tafoya, Tomasita 41

Tapia, Ernest 26 (male)

## 1940 census at Santa Clara:

Baca, Lucaria 21 / wife of Henry Baca Pablita's sister, not identified as a pottery maker, w/ son Henry Edgar 1 in 1940.

Velarde, Pablita 23 - single person head of household; artist; own studio; next to f & step mother.

## Pablita Velarde's Family

**Parents:**
Herman Velarde (1886 - )
1st wife Marianita Chavarria (1890 - 1921)
   Maria Legoria (1911 - 1984) = Pasqual Tafoya m. abt. 1933 <potter>
      Emilio Edward (abt 1930 - )
      Celestina "Celes" (abt. 1931 - )
      Michael (abt 1935 - )
   Rosita (1915 - 1992 ) = Paul David Tsosie m. abt. 1936 <potter>
      Donald
      Jonathan (1953-1990)
      Herman Paul (1934 - )
      Bertha Mae (1936-1998)
      Diane
      Betty
      Paula
   Marie Pablita (1916 - 2006) = Herbert Hardin m. 1942; div. 1957 <artist>
      Helen Hardin (1943-1984)
   Lucaria "Jane" Baca (1919 - 2011) married to Henry Baca <potter, figurines>
      Henry Edgar (April 1939 - )
      Velma
      Rozella
      Kathy
      Starr Tafoya (1952- )

      Velma
      Tim
2nd wife Rosita Gutierrez (1912 - )
   Victoria (1931 - )
   Teresa (1933 - ) = Tony Gutierrez
   Alfred (1936 - )

**Others potters perhaps in the Maisel mural:**
Margarite Tafoya (1904 - 2001)

www.ingramcontent.com/pod-product-compliance
Lightning Source LLC
Chambersburg PA
CBHW051922210526
45473CB00006B/2102